THE PLANNING OF
ROMAN ROADS
AND WALLS
IN NORTHERN BRITAIN

THE PLANNING OF
ROMAN ROADS
AND WALLS
IN NORTHERN BRITAIN

John Poulter

AMBERLEY

To David Breeze,
to whom the promotion and publication of this work
has owed so much

First published 2010

Amberley Publishing
Cirencester Road, Chalford,
Stroud, Gloucestershire, GL6 8PE

www.amberley-books.com

British Library Cataloguing in Publication Data.
A catalogue record for this book is available from the British Library.

ISBN 978-1-84868-548-2

Typesetting and origination by Amberley Publishing
Printed in Great Britain

CONTENTS

ACKNOWLEDGEMENTS

My studies of Roman roads and walls in northern Britain have gained immeasurably over the years from the interest, encouragement, advice, information, and, from time to time, correction of, from, and by many senior archaeologists in the field, including particularly Paul Bidwell, David Breeze, the late Charles Daniels, Nick Hodgson, the late Barri Jones and David Woolliscroft, for all of whose efforts I express my very considerable gratitude. I would also like to record my appreciation of much valuable information and advice that I have received along the way from, among others, Geoff Bailey, Arnaud Bertrand, Peter Checkland, Stephen Coleman, Donald Gordon, Bill Hanson, Birgitta Hoffmann, Rebecca Jones, Christopher Last, Michael Lewis, Peter McKeague and Pete Wilson. I am also grateful to Historic Scotland for commissioning my examination of the Antonine Wall and supporting the publication of my full archaeological reports in the form of a BAR monograph.

With regard to this book, my special thanks go to David Breeze who made the introduction to Peter Kemmis Betty about my work, and which then led directly to the publication of this volume by Amberley and my helpful working relationships with editors Tom Vivian and Jonathan Reeve. I would also like to thank Jennifer Laing for the copy editing, Jasper Hadman at Amberley for his assistance in the book's production, and James Pople at Amberley for the design and typesetting of the book. I am very grateful to Roger Oram for providing a number of the illustrations included within, and to the Archaeological Journal, Bedford Borough Council, Central Bedfordshire Council, the National Museum of Scotland and the Royal Archaeological Institute for permission to reproduce illustrations for which they hold the copyright. I am also very grateful to David Breeze and Barbara Tearle for kindly making the time to read drafts of my text and for suggesting numerous valuable improvements and corrections thereto, and also to Peter Checkland for agreeing to read and comment upon a draft of my Chapter 10, and making equally valuable suggestions upon that aspect of my work. Needless to say, any errors of fact or interpretation that may remain are, nonetheless, my own responsibility.

Finally, to the people who will read this book, I should declare that writing it has provided me with the opportunity to convey many of the thoughts and ideas that I had developed in concert with my growing experience, as I pursued my studies on the ground, in the libraries, and at the desk over many years. Without this publication, much of this thinking would have gone unrecorded. Hence I am very grateful indeed for the opportunity to present it here. I hope you will enjoy what I now put before you. I think you will find much within it to merit your attention and occasion your surprise.

John Poulter, Wing, Bucks
January, 2010

INTRODUCTION
THE ORIGINS OF THIS WORK

All my life I have been intrigued by roads, railways, and canals. Over and again, from one example to another, I have found myself asking: why were they built here and not there, what was involved in constructing them, and what remains to be seen of them today? And there are bigger questions too: why, in Britain, did we have a canal age before we had a railway age? Why, indeed, did we have a canal age at all?

Having been brought up in Leicester, near the course of the old Fosse Way, my interest in roads naturally extended to Roman roads. Like so many others before me, I was enormously impressed by the directness with which they strode across the countryside. How, I asked, did the Romans manage to follow such straight lines over such extended distances – far beyond what they could see physically? And how did the Roman surveyors who laid them out know where they should be going, and with such accuracy?

I was fascinated, too, with the thought that these Roman roads had been planned and constructed nearly 2,000 years ago, and yet that here they were, still with us, and with many of their lines still in use today. Just south of Leicester, past the village of Sharnford, the old Fosse Way became derelict, and I would wander up and down this neglected roadway to see what I might see. But how much of what I was seeing might be truly Roman? How much of the surface and the ditches on either side was authentically Roman, and how much was simply the standard superstructure of any old Leicestershire lane that just happened to have been kept open along the line of a Roman road?

After I had graduated from university, I moved to live in the north of England and then, for a short while, in Scotland. This gave me the opportunity to examine the courses of Roman roads across hills and moorlands where their remains had probably been undisturbed by agriculture or renovation since the Romans had left. Here, I felt, I was likely to be looking at things that really were Roman, and so I could see exactly how they were laid out on the ground. The stay in Scotland also gave me the opportunity to begin studying the military roads that had been set out in that country by General Wade and his successors in the eighteenth century, and to compare their planning and construction with that of their Roman predecessors some 1,600 years earlier.

My degree was in engineering, albeit not civil engineering. Nevertheless, my interest in Roman roads has always been that of an engineer – or, perhaps more specifically, that of a systems engineer. So my questions tended to be flavoured with a systems bent. For example, when the Romans were setting out their roads, what were their intentions, what was influencing their thinking, how did they organise themselves to build this, and why did they not adopt a particular course when it would seem to have been the obvious thing to do? And why have some parts of their roads survived to this day whilst elsewhere other parts of the same roads have disappeared without trace and cannot be found even by excavation? What factors will have been at work over the centuries to cause this phenomenon?

On business trips to and from Scotland I would, whenever possible, use the modern A68 road over Carter Bar. North of Hadrian's Wall the A68 follows much of the course of Dere Street, the former main Roman road up the eastern side of England into Scotland. From my repeated drives over this road I gradually gained the impression that much of the Roman road there had been planned from north to south. This surprised me. Like many people, I expect, I had assumed that Dere Street would have been planned from south to north, following the direction of the Roman army as it marched from England into Scotland some time in the second half of the first century AD. However, all I had was my hunch – which was that at least some parts of Dere Street had been set out in the opposite direction.

My question thus became: how could I demonstrate formally and objectively the direction in which the Roman surveyors may have been working when setting out the lines of their roads – and the line of Dere Street in particular? The method would not only have to be adequate to satisfy my own curiosity. If I were serious, it would have to be able to satisfy other students of Roman roads and the archaeological community in general.

It took me four years of intermittent rumination to hit upon a way of doing this, and, as I gained experience with it, the result of my quest gradually developed into more than just one method but a whole methodology for determining the directions in which Roman surveyors may have been working. It was the development of this methodology, coupled with the encouragement, advice, and support of several leading members of the archaeological profession that has led first of all to the publication of full archaeological reports of my work and then to this book, which is intended to be a more popular account of what I have investigated, observed, and found.

My work has not simply been confined to Roman roads. At the suggestion and invitation of the archaeologists David Breeze and Nick Hodgson, I extended my investigations beyond Dere Street to examine the courses of the two great Roman walls across northern Britain: Hadrian's Wall between the Tyne and the Solway, and the Antonine Wall between the Forth and the Clyde. The results proved to be full of surprises throughout, and I think it fair to claim that they may have added significantly to our understanding of these monuments – or at least to our thinking about them.

What follows, therefore, is an account of (a) my methodology for determining the directions in which Roman surveyors may have been working when laying out the lines of their roads and walls in northern Britain, and (b) the application of this methodology to Roman Dere Street, Hadrian's Wall (and the Vallum which runs behind it), and the Antonine Wall in Scotland. This account is laced with observations about Roman roads in general, particularly in the north of Britain, and about the processes of archaeological interpretation, which have been the subjects of a lifetime's study.

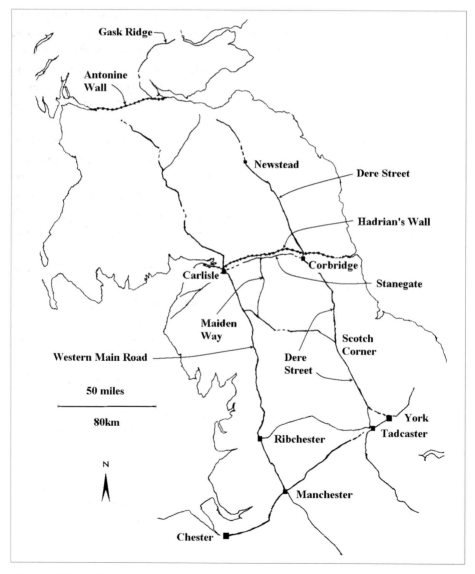

Figure 1: Principal Roman road network and the positions of Hadrian's Wall and the Antonine Wall in northern Britain.

1

SOME CHARACTERISTICS
OF ROMAN ROADS

Before describing the methodology, it will be useful to examine some characteristics of Roman roads – at least as they are to be found in Britain. Figure 1 indicates some of the Roman roads discussed in this section, which is chiefly concerned with northern Britain, and Plates 1 to 13 illustrate what can be seen of some of these roads at certain locations. For a more complete picture of the Roman road network in Britain see Ivan D. Margary's *Roman Roads in Britain*[1] or the Ordnance Survey Map of Roman Britain.

Roman roads are famous for being straight, but this does not apply to all of them, by any means. For instance, the so-called Stanegate Roman road (see Plates 7 to 9) which runs between Corbridge on the River Tyne and Carlisle on the River Eden does not appear in the main to follow any long-distance alignments, except perhaps at its western end. At that end, however, the style of planning is so different that I wonder if that part of the road had been set out later or under a separate command.

Similarly, the attractively named Maiden Way (see Plates 4 and 5), which runs over the hills from Kirby Thore near Appleby to Carvoran near Greenhead, by Hadrian's Wall, follows few alignments, especially over the higher ground. The Military Way (see Plate 6), which runs closely behind Hadrian's Wall, also shows little or no sign of long-distance alignments in its planning. However, this is hardly surprising since it had to run squeezed, in the main, between the Wall and the Vallum[2] and to service along the way the numerous forts, milecastles, and turrets with which Hadrian's Wall was equipped.

Dere Street itself (see Plates 10 to 13) seems to possess few signs of alignments when it crosses over the Cheviot Hills between England and Scotland. Over the hills, it mainly seems to have been laid out simply to follow the lie of the land.

The curious thing is not that Roman roads should curve when crossing hilly ground. It is that when they do so their planners seem to have abandoned all attempts at maintaining straight alignments for the entire span of the

---

1   Margary 1973.
2   For a description of the Vallum, which runs behind Hadrian's Wall, see Chapter 9.

hilly ground. They appear to have done this even when, it might seem, some stretches of the land in between would appear to have been amenable to the adoption of such alignments. It appears as though, on reaching hillier ground, the surveyors marking out the long distance alignments went back to base and left the construction teams to set out the course of the road as they fabricated it, on the spot.

It is not that the Roman surveyors were afraid of steep gradients. They would often run their roads up and down hillsides so steeply that they make even modern traffic pause for breath. What the Roman surveyors did not appear to do, to my knowledge in Britain at least, is apply the principle of a ruling or maximum gradient to their roads. The principle of a ruling gradient is something that was adopted for many of the later turnpike roads in Britain, and then by many of the railways. By setting a maximum gradient along all parts of a road (or railway), it meant that any wheeled vehicle travelling along it could be confident of setting out at one end and reaching the other end under its own motive power, without needing any assistance along the way. See Figures 2 and 3.

The adoption of a ruling gradient means that a road must twist and turn through hilly country and deep valleys – or else, particularly in the case of railways, resort to running through deep cuttings and high embankments or, in more severe cases, passing through tunnels or over lofty viaducts.

The Romans seem to have been well aware of the principle of a ruling gradient. They had to apply it, for instance, to the many aqueducts that they built to bring

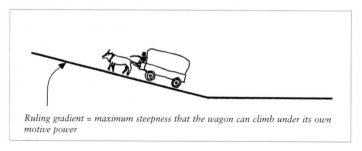

Ruling gradient = maximum steepness that the wagon can climb under its own motive power

Figure 2: Principle of a ruling gradient followed.

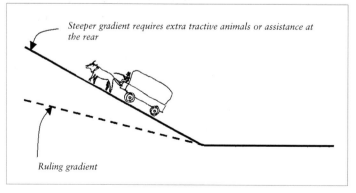

Steeper gradient requires extra tractive animals or assistance at the rear

Ruling gradient

Figure 3: Principle of a ruling gradient not followed.

water to their towns and their forts.[3] Along the ground, these aqueducts curve and meander through the landscape in order to maintain as constant an angle of fall as possible. In extreme cases – not in Britain, but in Italy and elsewhere in the Roman empire – their aqueducts would pass through tunnels or along spectacular viaducts looking much like extravagantly built railways. Yet for their roads the Romans seem to have preferred directness to ease of passage for wheeled vehicles. This seems to reflect the fact that the primary purpose of the roads was for military rather than civilian traffic – at least in Britain.

So, faced with such gradients, how did wheeled vehicles get along Roman roads in Britain, if they were going to need assistance, not just to get them up but also get them down the steeper slopes along the way? Some people have speculated that the Romans did not use wheeled transport north of Hadrian's Wall, but this does not seem to be correct. Parts of wheels and axles have been found at the fort of Newstead in Scotland, and much further north, wheel ruts were found at Ardoch fort,[4] whilst at Strageath and other forts north of Stirling, ramps were constructed up steep slopes. The efforts required to construct such ramps would appear to have been unwarranted if provision had not been required for wheeled traffic.[5] In addition, carts are mentioned in some of the letters that have come from the fort at Vindolanda. Admittedly, Vindolanda lies just south of Hadrian's Wall, but from one of the letters it is possible that some of the carts were being used to build the roads, and that therefore wheeled vehicles were being employed before the roads had been constructed. Hence the steepness of the inclines and declines along the roads themselves may not have been an insurmountable hindrance to their use for wheeled transport.

From correspondence with Michael Lewis, a specialist on Roman technology, my impression is that – in northern Britain at least – most wheeled vehicles would probably have travelled in convoy. This might have been primarily for security, but at least it meant that there would have been a ready supply of assistance available either from other members of each convoy or from troops escorting them, to help manhandle the carts and wagons up and down the steepest slopes.

This practice of travelling in convoy is well illustrated in the attached cartoon strip drawn by Roger Oram. Roger is a professional archaeologist and also editor of the magazine of the Arbeia Society, based in South Shields. He usually provides a cartoon strip for each issue of the magazine which is not only humorous but very well informed archaeologically. Thus although this cartoon has the cartoonist's hyperbole for amusing effect, it seems to me to portray quite well what travel would have been like in the Roman period in northern Britain, especially in the

---

3   For comprehensive accounts of Roman aqueducts and their planning see Hodge 1995 and Lewis 2001.

4   Breeze 1969-70, 122-3 with Plate 10.

5   Birgitta Hoffmann pers. comm.

aftermath of the conquest but before the Romans had been able to build their properly surfaced roads such as Dere Street, and were having to make do with temporary trackways and fords rather than bridges. See Figures 4a-c.[6]

Figure 4a: Roman travel in the early days after the conquest – setting out.

---

6   These clips are taken from *Arbeia* magazine No. 32, Summer 2005. Note that Roger has included in his cartoon strip some animals, such as the beaver and the lynx, which became extinct in Britain after the Roman period.

Figure 4b: Roman travel in the early days after the conquest – along the way.

Figure 4c: Roman travel in the early days after the conquest – approaching the fort.

Before leaving this chapter, it may be worth looking at what the construction of a Roman road looks like, once they did get round to building one properly. Plates 2 and 3 show a partial excavation of the western main Roman road to the north, on its way from Manchester to Carlisle (see Figure 1). The excavation was undertaken in the Lune Gorge, about 1½ miles (2.4km) south of the fort of Low Borrow Bridge, and about 3½ miles (5.6km) south of the modern settlement of Tebay. The foundation of the road is evident, solidly composed of large stones and boulders, and above it the gravelled upper surface can be seen to have quite a pronounced camber at this point.

In Italy, some of the Roman roads came to be surfaced with polygonal stones along certain stretches. However, in Britain, away from the approaches to towns and forts, Roman roads in general seem to have been surfaced only with gravel and small pebbles. The well-known stretch of paved road up Blackstone Edge near Littleborough, north-east of Manchester, is now considered not to be Roman, but this is discussed in more detail in Chapter 6.

Nevertheless, there may have been exceptions to the general pattern, even in Britain. Recent reports of excavations of the Military Way which runs behind Hadrian's Wall indicate that it may have been surfaced with stone slabs in places.[7]

---

7   Hodgson 2009, 97, 110.

2

ESTABLISHING BEARINGS AND MARKING OUT THE LINE ON THE GROUND

Roman roads seem, in Britain, to have been planned and built by the Roman army. It may be judged unlikely that the army would have been able to undertake these tasks when on campaign, aside from the necessity of establishing temporary routes and river crossings for their supplies and communications lines. Construction of the permanent road network is likely to have taken place in the period of consolidation and control over the conquered territory at some time afterwards, and my analysis of the planning and construction of Dere Street, described in Chapter 4, would appear to confirm this.

Elsewhere in the Roman Empire – for instance, in France and Spain – much of the main road building programme seems to have taken place up to 100 years or so after the provinces had been absorbed into the empire. From his study of the expansion of the Western Han Empire into Xinjiang province in China between 140 and 50 BC, Arnaud Bertrand of the Sorbonne University in Paris has formalised the typical steps of conquest into the following generic pattern:

1. attack
2. establish garrisons
3. occupy the major established settlements
4. colonise the land
5. build and secure the roads
6. construct fortifications[1]

although Arnaud stresses that for every conquest there will be circumstances which could cause this pattern to be modified in practice. However, to me this sequence certainly seems to comprise quite an appropriate template for the Roman conquest of northern Britain. Perhaps the most important point is to note

---

1 Noted from a Roman Archaeology Seminar delivered at Newcastle University in October, 2009. I am indebted to Arnaud Bertrand for permission to reproduce this model here. Arnaud has provided some bibliographical references supporting the construction of this model, which is drawn from the expansion of the Western Han Empire, and these are given in a separate section in the References for Chapter 2.

that the building of roads, and fortifications such as Hadrian's Wall, would have come late or last in the sequence.

It is possible, though, that some of the *planning* for the roads in northern Britain may have taken place well in advance of their construction. This is another finding from my work on Dere Street, which is discussed in Chapter 4. Indeed, it is possible that at least the outline planning of the Roman road network may have been part of the initial partitioning of the countryside for administration and control purposes, involving decisions about the dispositions of forts and towns at key locations, with the roads envisaged to be running as directly as possible between them. At the XXIst *Limes* Congress, a conference devoted to Roman frontiers that was held in 2009 at Newcastle upon Tyne, a number of reports were made that land stretching well beyond legionary fortresses appeared to have been marked out for specific purposes from the inception of the fortresses. This evidence came from a variety of Roman fortress sites in Europe, not just in Britain, and may be indicative of a much wider scale of planning of the landscapes by the Roman authorities than had been appreciated up to now.

Once the key locations in the Roman landscape had been decided – by whatever process – the Roman surveyors would then have been faced with two questions about how to lay out the lines of the roads between them. Taking any two locations, say A and B, and assuming that they would not have been intervisible, then the questions for the Roman surveyors would have been:

1. how to establish the bearing of B from A, so that they would know the broad direction in which to head the road;

2. where to lay out the course of the road upon the ground so as to follow the bearing as closely as possible in the face of obstacles such as river crossings, marshes, unacceptably steep inclines and declines, and possibly extensive woodland.

With regard to the first question, we can take the practical example of Dere Street. Scotch Corner is at the northern end of the Vale of York. It is where the line of the road coming northwards up the Vale of York divides, one arm turning north-west to cross the Pennines via the Stainmore Pass and then run up to Carlisle, whereas the other arm continues almost due north, heading eventually to Corbridge on the River Tyne (see Figure 1). Perhaps surprisingly, the planning of the line up the Vale of York appears to have set out from Tadcaster, not York. This is another of the findings from my study of Dere Street which is described and discussed in Chapter 4. Nevertheless, even though the Vale of York is very flat, Scotch Corner and Tadcaster are not intervisible. They are 42 miles (67.5km) apart. Yet the bearing of the first alignment set out from Tadcaster, which happened to be 24½ miles (39.4km) in length, was less than 2 degrees out from the exact bearing of Scotch Corner from Tadcaster. How might the Romans have achieved such apparent accuracy?

The Romans seem not to have left records of how they did this – or, if they have, their accounts have not yet been discovered. There are numerous writings by Roman land surveyors, but these are primarily concerned with techniques for measuring out land divisions accurately – for instance, for parcelling out areas of farmland set on sloping and curving hillsides – and then, perhaps understandably, propounding the surveyors' honesty as a profession![2] With regard to Roman roads, and in the absence of Roman explanations, two schools of thought have recently emerged in Britain about how the Roman surveyors may have established the initial bearings that their roads should take.

Hugh Davies proposes that the Romans first surveyed and mapped the entire landscape of an area, much as the Ordnance Survey has done for Britain in our times. From this, it would have been easy to calculate the bearing of B from A as a pair of displacements north-south and east-west.[3] See Figure 5. However, no such maps, if they existed, have come down to us.[4]

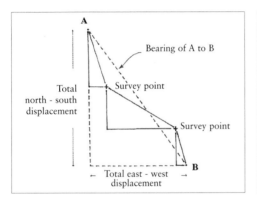 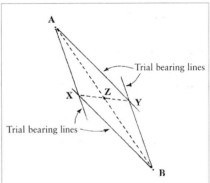

Left: *Figure 5:* Determining a bearing by means of a survey.

Right: *Figure 6:* Determining a bearing by geometrical construction. BY is parallel with AX, and BX is parallel with AY. Hence AXBY is a parallelogram. Thus the mid-point of the diagonal XY gives the exact bearing of B from A.

Instead, Michael Lewis proposes, largely on practical grounds, that the Romans are more likely to have established a bearing by geometrical construction. By setting out lines on the same projected bearings from both B and A, the intersections of these lines would form a parallelogram, and the half-way point of the diagonal between the intersections would give the exact bearing of B from A.[5] See Figure 6.

2   See Campbell 2000.
3   Davies 1998, 12-13; 2002, 40, 43-50.
4   David Breeze, pers. comm.
5   Lewis 2001, 232-3.

Michael Lewis suspects, though, that in practice the Romans may have used a variety of methods to establish the overall bearings for their roads, and I am inclined to agree with him on this. With regard to the line of Dere Street up the Vale of York, for example, the army itself and the people operating its supply chain to the north would have had a fairly good appreciation of the direction in which Scotch Corner lay, and it may not have been a priority for the Roman surveyors to have aligned Dere Street upon this point exactly. More likely, their priorities may have been to run up the Vale of York fairly centrally between the North York Moors to the east and the Dales to the west – both which would have been clearly visible on either hand – whilst avoiding the extensive flood plains of the River Ouse, and the rivers running into it: the Nidd, the Ure, and the Swale. Having reached Healam Bridge, south of Leeming, the Roman surveyors would then have been able to see, just, – especially if marked by a bonfire – the eminence upon which Scotch Corner stands, and at this point the alignment of Dere Street changes direction by two to three degrees and heads for Scotch Corner directly (see Figure 16). The resulting alignments might look dramatically accurate but the surveying process and objectives may well have been more prosaic.

What may be more impressive is the way that the Roman surveyors were able to follow their alignments over such long distances. There is abundant evidence that they were able to do this with astonishing accuracy, and to do so across river crossings, swamps, precipices, and, indeed, over multiple horizons. The planning of Dere Street itself appears to embody three dead straight alignments of more than 20 miles (32km), spanning several horizons. Elsewhere in Britain, Michael Lewis reports that the first 12½ miles (20km) of Stane Street, running between London and Chichester, is exactly aligned upon the east gate of Roman Chichester, a distance of nearly 60 Roman miles (88.7km) away, even though, because of the lie of the land, Stane Street then branches off this planning line at Ewell to run through Dorking, Ockley, and Borough Hill.[6] In this respect, we may note that the Outer German *Limes*,[7] between Walldürn and Haghof, runs almost dead straight for more than 50 miles (81km), apart from a one-mile (1.6km) deviation to avoid a steep valley. Michael Lewis reports that, along the southern 18 miles (29km) of this *Limes*, careful measurement has revealed that its mean deviation from a truly straight line was plus or minus only just over 6 feet (1.9 m).[8]

Again, ancient literature remains silent about how this was accomplished, but it seems probable that the Roman surveyors were able to achieve this straightness by marking out the line from horizon to horizon, or at least, high point to high point, using an instrument such as a *groma* to extend the same bearing from one

---

6   Lewis 2001, 238-42.

7   The Outer German *Limes* (pronounced Leem-es) is the Roman frontier line constructed in Germany at the end of the reign of Antoninus Pius (AD 138-61).

8   Lewis 2001, 242-5.

point to the next.[9] Perhaps we should remember that, without modern pollution, long distance visibility may have been better in Roman days and more akin to that in the highlands of Scotland in our own times, where, on clear days, the neighbouring mountains can still look deceptively close.

To return to the planning process, once the overall direction of point B from point A had been established – whether accurately or approximately – the Roman surveyors would then have been faced with the second question: how to plot the course of their road across the intervening countryside. Once again, there are two schools of thought about how this might have been accomplished.

Hugh Davies, believing that the Romans would already have surveyed the countryside, including its marshes, woodlands, rivers and crags, considers that the road planners would then have plotted out the course of their road on their maps so as to avoid these obstacles and take advantage of the best lie of the land in between. He believes that the surveyors would then have transferred this course to the ground by scaling up measurements from the maps and pacing them out on the ground as offsets from their original survey lines. See Figure 7. Furthermore, Hugh Davies considers that the easiest way to execute this transfer from the map to the ground would be to plot the course of the road in straight lines, and that this mechanism therefore explains the straightness that many Roman roads possess.[10]

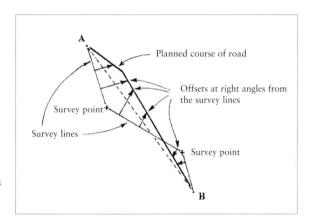

Figure 7: Setting out the line of a Roman road by means of offsets from the survey lines.

Michael Lewis, in contrast, believes that the Roman surveyors worked out the courses of their roads directly on the ground, by observing the landscapes before them and adjusting their lines to suit. From my many years' experience of following Roman roads on the ground, I am inclined to agree with Michael

9   Lewis 2001, 124-33, 217-20.
10 Davies 1998, 13-15; 2002, 50-52.

Lewis's position on this. Indeed, the belief that they did work in this way underpins the methodology I have devised for determining the direction in which Roman surveyors may have been working when setting out the lines of their roads, and which I will now describe in the next chapter.

3

A METHODOLOGY FOR DETERMINING THE DIRECTION OF PLANNING OF ROMAN ROADS

Before describing the methodology, I should make it clear that it was not developed by me to prove that I was right – in other words, to demonstrate that my hunch about some of the planning of Dere Street was correct. The methodology was developed in order to offer a means of detecting as objectively as possible the direction or directions in which the Roman surveyors may have been working when setting out the lines of their roads upon the ground. It was intended that the methodology should be usable by any researcher on Roman roads and that its findings should be credible to the archaeological community as a whole. As it happens, application of the methodology to Dere Street did indicate that my hunch about the planning of parts of that road – as described in the Introduction – had been correct, but this was a bonus that came in retrospect, not as a prior condition.

The methodology comprises a number of ways – a toolkit of diagnostic indicators, in fact – that can be used in combination to help detect the direction in which Roman surveyors may have been working. The first of these ways is what I call the 'best field of view' test. I came to it, eventually, in May 2004, by deciding to concentrate on two well-known features of Roman roads:

a) their straightness, often followed rigidly for many miles;
b) their tendency, when changing direction, to do so on high ground.

How might these, I asked, be used to diagnose the direction in which a Roman surveyor may have been working? My assumption at first was that a Roman surveyor, following an alignment but seeking to change direction, would maintain course on the alignment up to the top of a convenient hill offering good views both forwards and backwards and would then set out a new alignment from there. However, it occurred to me that most hills in Britain have fairly rounded tops, and that although good views into the distance might be offered from their summits, the nearer ground below the hill is often invisible from its topmost point. My feeling, then, was that a Roman (or, indeed, any) surveyor would be more comfortable when setting out a new alignment if they had a view not only into the distance but over the middle ground and the foreground as well. Hence my surmise developed – that a Roman surveyor

Figure 8: Changing alignment at the brow of a hill.

Figure 9: Basis of the diagnostic test.

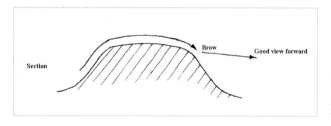

Figure 9a: Surveyor proceeding over a hill to a convenient brow.

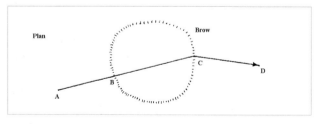

Figure 9b: Surveyor working from left to right.

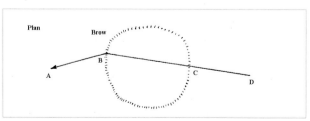

Figure 9c: Surveyor working from right to left.

would be inclined to extend their existing alignment across the top of a hill until they came to a convenient brow from which they could see not just the far distance but the middle and near ground as well, before they then set out a new alignment into the landscape.

This arrangement is illustrated imaginatively in Figure 8, and in section and plan in Figure 9. Looking down on the hilltop from above, as shown in Figure 9b, it can be seen that a Roman surveyor working from left to right might thus follow their existing alignment from A to B and over the top of the hill to the brow at C before changing direction towards D. Conversely, a Roman surveyor working from right to left might follow their existing alignment from D to C and over the top of the hill to the brow at B before changing direction towards A, as shown in Figure 9c. It follows that by (a) identifying the precise spot at which the Roman surveyor will have been standing when setting out a new alignment, and then (b) assessing the best field of view at that spot, it should be possible to determine the direction in which the Roman surveyor is likely to have been working when setting out the new alignment. Thus at point C in Figure 9b, it can be expected that there would be a fine view towards D but a very limited view, if any, towards point B, whereas in Figure 9c there would be a fine view towards A from B, but only a limited view at best from B to C.

This 'best field of view' test will only work if the Roman surveyors did indeed follow their existing alignments rigidly over the tops of hills until they come to their points of turn, and if they then turned at single points rather than in gradual curves. However, the evidence on the ground is that this was their normal practice. Where the Romans diverged from this practice, or where they abandoned straight alignments for their roads altogether (as along Dere Street, for instance, where it passes through the Cheviot Hills – to be described in the next chapter), this 'best field of view' test cannot diagnose the direction of working.

Another test that I developed is the 'left bank, right bank' one, which can be applied in situations where a Roman road changes direction near a stream or river crossing. Changes of direction of Roman roads occur less frequently at stream or river crossings than they do on high ground, but they do happen. On page 28, Figure 10 shows an artist's impression of such a situation, and Figure 11 shows it in section and plan.

It can be seen in Figure 11a that a Roman surveyor working from left to right and approaching a river crossing would have a far better view of the ground ahead from the left bank, before he crossed the river, than he would have once he had crossed over. Once he had crossed over he would be forced to look uphill and be able to see only a short way in front. Hence it is likely that a Roman surveyor approaching a stream or river crossing and wanting to change the direction of his road would set out the new alignment on the left bank when working from left to right, and on the right bank when working from right to left, as shown in Figure 11b. Unlike the 'best field of view' test, this test can be applied simply by

Figure 10: Changing alignment before a river crossing.

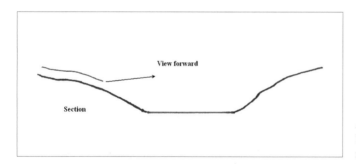

Figure 11a: Best view before crossing over the river.

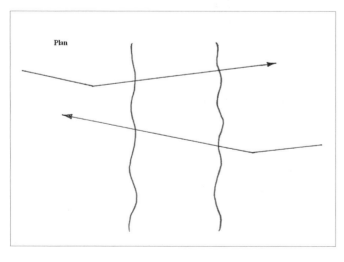

Figure 11b: Directions of planning at river crossings.

checking where alignments change on a map – although I would caution that it is advisable to verify the view on the ground whenever possible. With the 'best field of view' test, on the other hand, my experience shows that it is always *essential* – unless it should be utterly impractical – to visit the spot where the alignment changes and to assess the field of view by eye on the ground. I have found that trying to estimate what would be the best field of view from a map can sometimes be surprisingly misleading.

Another indicator that can be used to diagnose the likely direction of working can be the existence of a prominent feature in the landscape, such as an unusually shaped hilltop. If the Roman road appears to be aligned upon such a feature, and especially if there should be a fairly featureless landscape in the opposite direction, then the probability is that the Roman surveyor will have been working towards the feature rather than away from it. See Figure 12. Working backwards from a prominent feature is possible but less natural than working towards it.

Figure 12: Surveyors using a prominent feature as a sighting point.

Another indicator, which emerged from my study of Dere Street, is that the minimum change of angle that the Roman surveyors seemed able to achieve when adjusting the directions of their alignments appears to have been about 2 to 3 degrees. I do not know why this should have been so for the Romans, but what it means is that if two alignments have an angle between them which is less than this, then these alignments are likely to have been planned from opposite ends towards where they meet. Their point of intersection is unlikely to have been where a change of direction had been planned. See Figure 13. This is especially likely to have been the case if the point of intersection should not be on a brow or should not otherwise appear to have been an opportune place from which to plan a change of alignment.

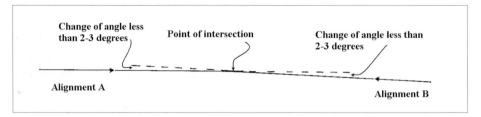

Figure 13: A change of direction of less than 2-3 degrees is likely to be the result of an intersection of alignments set out from opposite directions.

Another indicator can be a change of alignment where a destination or a prominent feature in the landscape first comes into view. On Dere Street there are examples of this just south of Healam Bridge and just north of the crossing of the River Swale at Catterick Bridge. In the case of the former, it suggests that the surveyor was working from south to north towards Healam Bridge (see Figure 16) whilst in the case of the latter it appears that the surveyor would have been working from north to south, from Scotch Corner towards Catterick Bridge (see Figure 23).

In addition to indicators such as these, there can be clues that can be derived from individual situations along the line of the road. With regard to Dere Street, for instance, the first planning line of 24½ miles is exactly aligned upon Tadcaster. In theory a Roman surveyor standing at the north end of this alignment could have determined the exact bearing of Tadcaster from where he was standing by using one of the methods described in Chapter 2, and then worked towards it from north to south. However, to have done so would have been extremely laborious and seemingly pointless. It appears vastly more likely that the surveyor would have worked from south to north here, setting out from Tadcaster on his chosen bearing, and then adjusting it slightly as Healam Bridge came into view.

It will be apparent that none of these indicators can produce conclusive proof of the directions in which the Roman surveyors would have been working. The indicators are based upon suppositions of what would have been convenient in practice for surveyors working out the course of their roads on the ground, and using the habits which evidence shows them to have employed regularly, such as following straight alignments rigidly up hill and down dale, and then turning at singular points on the ground rather than making gentle curves.

It might be asked how the application of these indicators could be made more rigorous. One way of doing this which I have used on both Dere Street and on

Hadrian's Wall has been to divide the decipherment of the surveyors' directions of working into sectors – such as from the Vale of York to Scotch Corner, from Scotch Corner to the River Tyne, and north of the Cheviot Hills, etc. – and then to analyse the directions of working for each of these sectors separately. Only when each of them had been analysed individually did I then bring the results together to see if a coherent picture might emerge from end to end. If my analyses had been fundamentally flawed, then bringing the results together would almost certainly have produced a chaotic and incoherent overall picture. Instead, the opposite happened: coherent pictures emerged for the planning of both Dere Street and Hadrian's Wall. I believe that what I will be describing in the following chapters can therefore be treated with some confidence.

Nevertheless, interpreting the directions of planning is not easy, and it is compounded by a complication introduced by the Romans themselves. As is well illustrated by the example of Dere Street, it appears that the Romans did not plan the lines of their roads in one pass. Typically, it seems, they would travel over the landscape first to mark out a framework of long-distance alignments. Then they would make another pass – or sometimes several passes – over the landscape to mark out deviations from the long-distance alignments in order to meet local objectives. These objectives might be to avoid an area of marshy ground, or to work down to a suitable crossing of a major river, or to diverge to service a town or fort that might have been established after the initial long-distance alignment had been set out. These deviations would often return to the initial long-distance alignments after achieving their objectives, but the crucial point is that these deviations would often be planned in different directions from those of the long-distance planning. See Figures 14a and 14b.

Figure 14a: Roman road planning process: long-distance alignments set out first, shown here working from left to right.

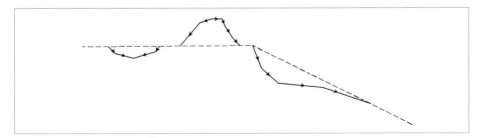

Figure 14b: Roman road planning process: deviations set out from the long-distance alignments in a variety of directions.

The result is that after diagnosing the probable directions of planning of the road, as built, one can be faced with a situation such as that depicted in Figure 15. Trying to make sense of a picture like this can take a long time. It is only when one spots, for instance, that small parts of the road are exactly aligned with other parts several miles away that one begins to identify the long distance framework of alignments underpinning the road as built and to understand what the Roman surveyors may have been doing, some 1900 years ago. Although it took several weeks for me to visit and assess the best field of view at every point where Dere Street and Hadrian's Wall (and the Vallum) change direction, it took me many more months – and, indeed, years – afterwards to make sense of their planning from my observations.

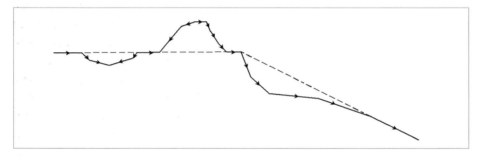

Figure 15: Roman road as built.

And this, perhaps, raises a point with which to conclude this chapter. I hope that readers will feel encouraged to apply the methodology themselves, but if they do so there is one crucial point that must not be overlooked. When trying to decipher the direction of planning of a Roman road or wall, it is most important that the observations of the best field of view, and any other indicators of the possible ways of working, should be made without any preconceptions. As soon as you start to develop a conviction that the Roman surveyors may have been working in a certain direction, you will start to introduce bias into your observations. Unavoidably, all of your observations will have an element of subjectivity about them anyway. What this means, therefore, is that your observations should all be made first, and as objectively as possible, before attempts at interpretation begin. You can always return to double check your observations if your subsequent analyses throw up questions, but if you start with preconceptions about what the Romans were doing, you will run a high risk of only observing what you want to believe. My surveys of Dere Street, Hadrian's Wall, and the Antonine Wall in Scotland all unearthed several discoveries that were completely unexpected, by all concerned, and I believe that these arose because in each case I began by making my observations with an entirely open mind and simply recording what I saw, with no preconceptions.

CASE STUDY 1: THE PLANNING OF ROMAN DERE STREET

Armed with the initial components of my methodology, and developing the rest as I gained experience, I set out to apply it to the planning of Dere Street. Dere Street is the name that we give nowadays to the chain of Roman roads that formed the Romans' eastern main line of communication up through the north of England and into Scotland. I examined the planning of this chain of roads from the Vale of York up to the Roman fort at Newstead, near Melrose, in Scotland. See Figure 1.

I began by identifying on maps every change of alignment along the course of Dere Street. Fortunately, this course has been fully established and is marked on current Ordnance Survey maps. However, to avoid being misled by deviations introduced by modern road improvements, I cross-checked my identified points with the first edition Ordnance Survey maps, which date from the mid-nineteenth century in this area. I then visited each of these turning points to assess the best field of view, and any other features that might indicate the direction of planning. I made these observations in 2004 and 2005, but the analysis of them continued into 2006 and the final version of the full archaeological report was not completed until shortly before it was published in 2009 as part of a BAR Monograph, Number 492.[1]

To begin with, my work was exploratory. The key questions were:

- would the methodology prove to work, as applied to Dere Street?
- if it did, what might it tell us about the planning of that chain of roads?

As it became apparent that the methodology was working, and producing coherent pictures of how the planning had been undertaken, the emphasis shifted from the first question to the second. It even became possible to interpret some of the sequences in which not only the planning but also the construction of Dere Street had taken place. The full details of my observations and analyses of each section of the route are intensively laid out in the Monograph, and the reader who wishes to examine my arguments in full should refer to that document. For the purposes of this book, I will offer a summary of my findings and conclusions for the general reader.

---

1 Poulter 2009, 3-31.

It appears that the planning of Dere Street commenced with the setting out of a chain of three long-distance alignments from Tadcaster across the Vale of York to Scotch Corner. See Figure 16.[2] The fact that the Roman planning appears to have started at Tadcaster rather than York is one of the surprises to come from my work. It is not known what kind of installation the Romans had at Tadcaster at that time. Later on, a small Roman town came to be sited there, reportedly with the name of Calcaria, and it is possible that a military installation had preceded it at this location.[3]

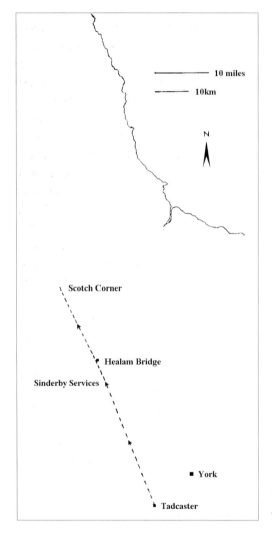

Figure 16: The initial planning for Dere Street: setting out the alignments from Tadcaster to Scotch Corner.

---

2   In all the maps, the arrows indicate the diagnosed direction of planning.

3   David Breeze, pers. comm., observes that if the planning of Dere Street had indeed started at Tadcaster, it would strongly imply the existence of a fort there at that time.

The three long-distance alignments up the Vale of York had lengths of:

- 24½ miles (39.4 km) from Tadcaster to near where Sinderby Services was located until recently;
- 2⅝ miles (4.2km) from there to New Inn farm, just north of the Roman site at Healam Bridge;
- 15 miles (24.1km) from New Inn Farm to Scotch Corner.

Interestingly, it appears that, of the first of these three long-distance alignments, only the northernmost tip came to be used by Dere Street, when it was eventually built. However, this tip, from near Dishforth to Sinderby Services, is exactly aligned upon Tadcaster, more than 20 miles away to the south. In my experience, this cannot be a coincidence, and as already discussed in Chapter 3, it appears considerably more likely that the planning would have started in Tadcaster rather than terminated there.

The indication that the Roman planning appears to have started at Tadcaster rather than York offers an important clue about the date when these initial alignments may have been set out. It is generally believed that the Roman conquest of northern Britain commenced around AD 71, once the emperor Vespasian had stabilised his position in Rome. Soon after this date, as part of the campaign, it is understood that the Ninth Legion was moved from Lincoln to a new base at York, and it seems scarcely credible that the planning of the main road to the north would not have started from York once that place had become established as a legionary fortress. Hence these three planning lines from Tadcaster up the Vale of York appear likely to have been laid out in the immediate aftermath – or even as part – of the initial Roman advance.[4]

At Scotch Corner, the planning lines divided. See Figure 17 on page 36. One branch went off to the north-west, to cross the Pennine Hills via the Stainmore Pass and link up with the western main Roman line coming up from Chester and Manchester at Brougham, near Penrith, before continuing up to Carlisle. I have not surveyed this arm of the Roman road system, and so I do not know the direction of planning over the Stainmore Pass, nor which line reached Penrith first – the one coming up from Manchester or the one coming over from Scotch Corner. However, we do know from dendrochronological (tree-ring) dating that the Romans had begun to construct a fort at Carlisle in the winter of AD 72-3.

Back at Scotch Corner, the other arm of the planning appears to have been set out to run almost due north for some 24 miles (38.6km) to where the small village of Esh now stands upon a steep-sided hill running east-west in County Durham. Here the Roman surveyors made a turn of about 30 degrees towards the north-

4   They also may indicate an earlier foundation date for Tadcaster than York (David Breeze pers. comm.).

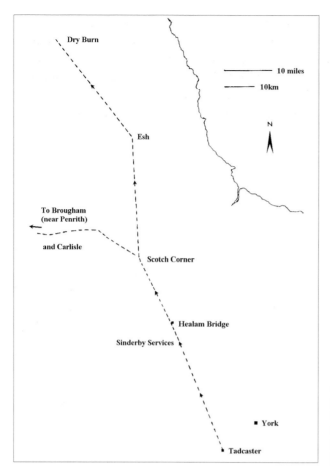

Figure 17: The initial planning for Dere Street: setting out the alignments from Scotch Corner to the Dry Burn, north of the River Tyne.

west and another alignment appears to have been set out for a further 26 miles (41.8km). This terminated at a not particularly significant stream called the Dry Burn, some 7-8 miles (12km) north of the River Tyne.

The indications of the direction of planning of these long-distance alignments are consistently from south to north across the Vale of York and from Scotch Corner up to the Dry Burn. Moreover, the style of long-distance planning is the same to both the north and the south of Scotch Corner. It is therefore possible that this planning was carried out by the same team of Roman surveyors and as part of a single exercise. If so, this may offer an indication of the extent of the Roman advance on the eastern side of the Pennines in the initial stages of its conquest, possibly corresponding with the founding of the fort at Carlisle in the west.

It should be noted that all that I have described so far relates to the planning process, and only to that part of the process that relates to the setting out of the framework of long-distance alignments. As will be seen below, I believe that at this time little or none of Dere Street as we know it will have been constructed on the ground.

The next stage of the planning of Dere Street seems to have occurred further north, as far as I can tell, at the point in time when the Romans had settled upon their preferred route through the Cheviot Hills. See Figure 18. Except for one short length, this route through the Cheviot Hills does not employ straight alignments: the road just seems to have been laid out to follow the lie of the land. Hence, as explained in Chapter 3, I cannot diagnose the direction of planning here.

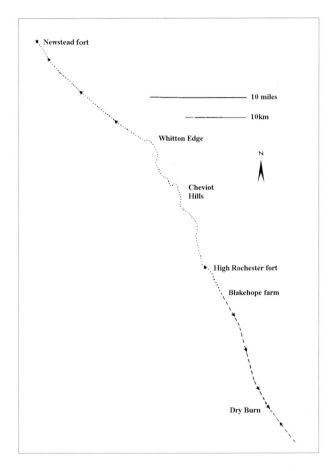

Figure 18: Further planning of Dere Street: from the Dry Burn through the Cheviot Hills to Newstead by the River Tweed. The only long-distance alignments appear to run from Blakehope farm to the Dry Burn.

However, south of the Cheviot Hills, from near Blakehope farm, where a Roman fort or fortlet came to be sited at some time, a chain of long-distance alignments can be detected that appears to have been planned from north to south. See Figure 18 again. It was along this stretch of the road that I had first gained the impression that at least some parts of Dere Street had been planned from north to south, and the best fields of view at each change of alignment here appear to confirm – objectively – that my hunch had been correct. The style of planning here, though, is quite different from that further south. The alignments are shorter, and, moreover, they appear to incline, step by step, so as to make a junction at the Dry Burn with the line coming up from the south. They therefore appear to have been planned later than the line coming up from Esh. However, the two lines did not manage to meet exactly at the Dry Burn, and the implications of this are discussed below.

In the meantime, to the north of the Cheviot Hills, Dere Street begins its long descent to the fort at Newstead from a scarp called Whitton Edge. See Figure 18 once more. At first glance this descent may appear to be in a straight line, and most people who have written about this stretch of Dere Street in the past have stated that its course was aligned upon the Eildon Hills which form such a prominent landmark, in full view ahead. In fact, careful observation reveals that neither statement is correct. The course of Dere Street down from Whitton Edge proves, on close inspection, to be a series of short straights which, cumulatively, combine to curve the line around to the north so as to cross the River Teviot and the Jed Water near their confluence and then to round the corner of the River Tweed by St Boswells before running up to the fort at Newstead. I could detect no long-distance alignment along this stretch of Dere Street. Rather, it seems likely that the Romans may have been laying out the course of the road here as they were building it, one stretch at a time.

The course of the final stretch of Dere Street towards Newstead may remain to be fully confirmed. However, as the line of what appears to be Dere Street approaches the south gate of the fort at Newstead, it can be seen on aerial photographs that it executes a dog-leg right in front of the fort's gate. It seems most unlikely that the road would have been planned to do this. However, the gateway showing on the aerial photographs belongs to that of the second, Domitianic, fort on the site, which is believed to have been founded after AD 86.[5] It therefore appears possible that its predecessor, an earlier Flavian fort that was probably founded in the late 70s or early 80s AD, may have been constructed on a slightly different alignment, and that the course of Dere Street had been planned to align with where the gateway of this earlier fort had been positioned.

If this deduction should be correct, it would date not only the planning but also the construction of Dere Street here to some time before AD 86-7. The argument for this is that if Dere Street had only been planned but not built before the Domitianic fort had been constructed, then it would have been simple to have altered the alignment of Dere Street so that it would run straight up to the new fort's gate. The fact that a dog-leg had to be inserted right in front of the gate suggests that this final part of Dere Street had already been constructed by then, and that therefore the dog-leg was the result of a re-alignment when the Domitianic fort came to be built.

If this should be so, then it is possible that this final stretch of Dere Street,[6] from the Cheviot Hills to Newstead, may have been the first part of Dere Street to

5   Information derived from an unpublished report by Simon Clarke 29-06-07, based upon the University of Bradford's excavations at the site.

6   That is, the final stretch in my survey. Dere Street itself appears to have continued well beyond Newstead and to have been heading towards Edinburgh and the Firth of Forth. See Figure 1.

have been constructed between the Vale of York and the fort at Newstead. Further south, there are grounds for suspecting that little or no parts of Dere Street as we know it (i.e. as mapped) were constructed before AD 86.

Before returning further south, though, we need to examine the possible sequence of events at the Dry Burn, where the alignments coming down from the north fail to make an exact junction with the alignment coming up from the south. It seems as though the Roman surveyors working down from the north were aware of the need to make a junction at the Dry Burn, but not quite sure where it should be. Perhaps the marker at the end of the line coming up from the south had been mislaid. If so, this could suggest that there might have been some interval of time between the two planning phases. Alternatively, the surveyors coming down from the north might have felt that the line coming up from the south would have crossed the Dry Burn at an awkward place, and that they needed to aim for a crossing point further to the west.

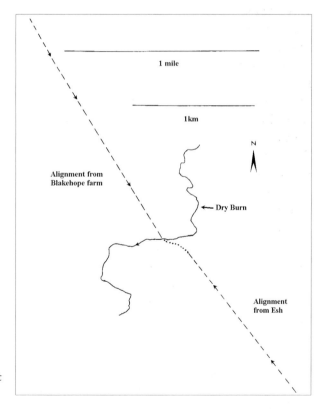

Figure 19: Correcting curve at the crossing of the Dry Burn.

In either case, a curve would need to have been inserted into the line of the road in order to form the junction, and the fact that this curve was made on the southern side of the Burn suggests that this may have been the part of the road that was built last. See Figure 19. The curve can be seen plainly on the ground today, and there appears to be little doubt that it was original. Thus it appears that whilst the alignment from the north may have been planned later than the alignment coming up from the south, the sequence of the construction of Dere Street, when it reached this point, may well have been in the opposite order.

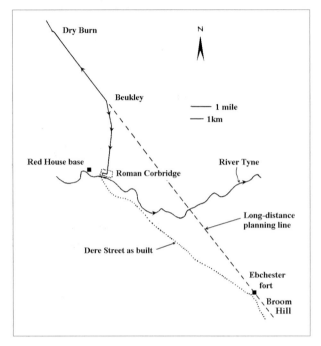

Figure 20: Deviation of Dere Street to run to Corbridge.

Some 4¼ miles (6.8km) south-east of the Dry Burn, the line of Dere Street turns abruptly southwards at Beukley to head to the crossing of the River Tyne below the Roman site at Corbridge. See Figure 20. This turn clearly represents a deviation from the long-distance alignment from Esh, and since the two small changes of direction along the route of this branch to Corbridge are both south-facing, it implies that this deviation was planned here from north to south. However, it is believed that Corbridge was not established until AD 86 or shortly afterwards, in concert with the start of the Roman withdrawal from northern Scotland at around that time.[7] Before then the Roman base on the north side of the Tyne had been located about a mile or so to the west, at Red House. Yet there is no indication on the ground that Dere Street had ever been aligned or constructed upon the Red House site. It thus appears that it would not have been possible to set out the course of Dere Street – or, of course, to build it – until the site of Corbridge had been chosen. Hence it appears that this deviation to Corbridge was probably not set out or built until AD 86 or later.

---

7   David Breeze pers. comm.

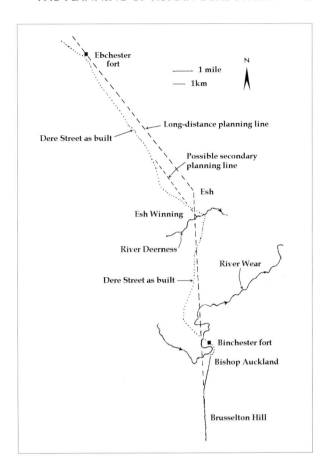

Figure 21: Protracted deviations and line-of-sight planning between Ebchester and Binchester forts.

This deviation to Corbridge returns to the long-distance alignment from Esh at a point on Broom Hill, above the Roman fort at Ebchester, but then Dere Street, as built, almost immediately deviates from the alignment again. In fact it appears that the Romans may have set out a second long-distance planning line from near here to run slightly to the south of the original long-distance alignment to Esh. This secondary line would have met the long-distance alignment coming up from Scotch Corner at or close by the crossing of the River Deerness, near Esh Winning. See Figure 21. If so, the Romans then deviated from this second line, too, to build the course of Dere Street south of Ebchester in a series of short straights which appear to have been set out on a line-of-sight basis, i.e. the ends of each short straight would have been intervisible. It seems as though the Roman construction teams may have lost track of the original planning framework to some extent or else were having to work in dense woodland and so were being forced to re-survey the course of Dere Street as they went along. For this reason I am inclined to think that this part of Dere Street may have been the last or one of the last portions to be completed. However, I have no other evidence for this supposition.

South of the River Deerness, the original long-distance alignment from Scotch Corner to Esh had the misfortune to cross the River Wear at least three times. The Roman construction teams solved this problem by deviating to the west of the Wear Valley until they reached the bank of the river opposite where the fort of Binchester came to be sited. They then crossed the River Wear and skirted the eastern side of the Wear by Bishop Auckland until they were able to re-join the original long-distance alignment below Brusselton Hill. See Figure 21 again. Again, some of the planning here appears to have been carried out on a line-of-sight basis, and I am inclined to think that much of this part of Dere Street was constructed late in the process too – possibly even after AD 105, based upon the following evidence from Piercebridge.

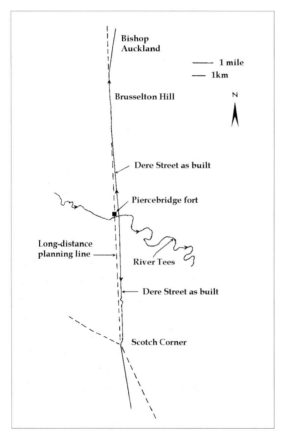

Figure 22: Deviation to cross the River Tees at Piercebridge.

At Piercebridge, to the south of Brusselton Hill, the Romans were able to find a suitable crossing place for Dere Street over the River Tees that was only a few hundred yards east of the long-distance planning line, at the back of the George Hotel – or, more accurately, Piercebridge Cottage. Hence the deviation here was a small one. See Figure 22. On the north bank of the river, on this deviation, excavators found pottery under the earliest surface of Dere Street which led them to believe that the road had not been constructed there until AD 100 or later.[8]

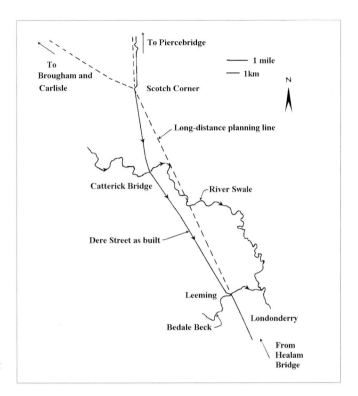

Figure 23: Deviation to cross the River Swale at Catterick Bridge.

South of Scotch Corner, it is apparent that the Romans were also forced to put in a deviation to Catterick Bridge. See Figure 23. The reason is readily apparent. Near Catterick the long-distance planning line from Healam Bridge to Scotch Corner would have run along the flood plain of the River Swale for some 2½ miles (4km). This meant that the road would have had to cross the river several times if this course had been followed unswervingly. In order to avoid this prospect, the Roman surveyors appear to have set out a deviation from Scotch Corner to cross the Swale about half a mile upstream, opposite Catterick Bridge, before re-joining the original alignment from Healam Bridge at Leeming. From observations of the best fields of view, this deviation appears to have been set out entirely from north to south.

Where this deviation returns to the original alignment at Leeming, it does so with a reverse curve, like that at the Dry Burn, and this again offers an interesting insight into the possible sequence of planning and construction here. See Figure

---

8   Cool and Mason 2008, 96.

23 again. It will be clear that the deviation will have been planned after the long-distance alignment. It will also be clear that if the surveyor of the deviation had been planning to return to the long-distance alignment at the crossing of Bedale Beck at Leeming, then he got it slightly wrong. However, if he had extended his slightly faulty alignment past the Bedale Beck to re-join the original alignment further south at, say, Londonderry, then his mistake would have been covered up and remained unnoticed. Why might he not have been able to do this? One probable reason could be that the road up from Healam Bridge to Leeming had already been built by the time that the surveyor was setting out his deviation. If so, he would have had no option but to put in the reverse curve to join the original line at Bedale Beck.

This is one of several instances along the course of Dere Street which incline me to think that in general the deviations were only planned when the road was being constructed. In principle, the surveyors of the original long-distance alignments could, after setting them out, then have worked backwards along their newly created planning lines, marking out deviations from them to avoid the obstacles that had been spotted along the way. Thus they could have presented the construction teams with a fully worked out line on which to build the road when circumstances permitted. However, along Dere Street, the standard of surveying of the deviations is noticeably less skilful than that of the long-distance alignments, suggesting that different teams were involved, and from my analyses above it appears unlikely that deviations to places such as Corbridge could have been set out when the long-distance alignments were being planned.

The southernmost deviation of Dere Street appears to have been intended to divert the road from the long-distance alignment at a point near Dishforth so as to terminate it at York rather than Tadcaster. I have not tried to diagnose the direction of planning here because the flatness of the countryside is likely to render the 'best field of view' test unreliable. See Figure 24. However, the original long-distance alignment from Tadcaster to Sinderby Services would have passed just to the west of the centre of Boroughbridge. A little further to the west of this, where the A1 road now crosses the River Ure, Mike Bishop recently excavated an early Roman military station which appeared to have been located beside a crossing of the river. It is possible that this would have been part of one of the temporary trackways and crossing-points with which, as suggested in Chapter 2, the Roman army on campaign may have had to make do until properly built roads and bridges could be constructed.

Mike Bishop's analysis of the dating evidence from the military station is that it may have continued in use until the mid 80s AD.[9] It is considered likely to have been abandoned as soon as the Romans had constructed their road from York to join the planning line to Scotch Corner near Dishforth. This road from York,

---

9   Bishop 2005, 218-9.

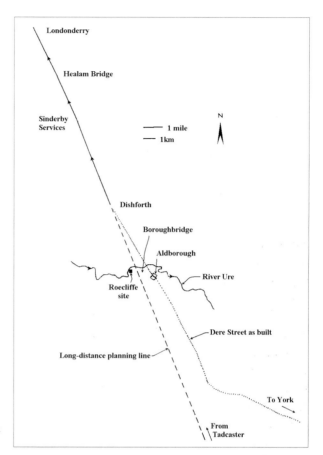

Figure 24: Deviation of Dere Street, as built, from Dishforth to York.

now considered part of Dere Street, crossed the Ure at Aldborough, conveniently closer to York than the station west of Boroughbridge, whilst still avoiding the floodplain of the River Ouse. It may be assumed that it would have been more substantially bridged, too, than the earlier crossing point. Hence it appears that this final deviation in the course of Dere Street may not have been constructed before the mid 80s AD.

If these analyses should be correct, we are faced with the prospect that there may have been a gap of 30 years or more in some places between the setting out of the original long-distance alignments of Dere Street and the completion of its construction. This may come as a shock to many peoples' preconceptions. In one of the letters from the Roman fort of Vindolanda, dating to about AD 105, a soldier complains about the bad state of the roads between Catterick and Vindolanda.[10] This usually causes people to express surprise that Roman roads should be in such poor condition so soon after they had been built. A more

---

10 Vindolanda letter 343.

likely explanation, as I believe I have shown, is that parts of Dere Street had not been completed by that time, and that in places the Romans were still having to manage with the temporary trackways and river crossings envisaged in Chapter 2. The Stanegate Roman road from Corbridge to Vindolanda may not have been completed by this date either, as I will discuss in the next chapter.

This apparently extended gestation period for Dere Street will certainly dismay those who – following Tacitus's account of the exploits of his father-in-law – have glibly attributed all of the elements of the Roman conquest of northern Britain to Agricola, including giving him credit for determining the line of Dere Street up the eastern side of the country. If the foregoing analysis of the dating should be correct, Agricola would have had little or no connection with either the course or the construction of Dere Street. Much of its line appears to have been set out well before he became governor of Britain in AD 77 or 78, and most of it seems not to have been built until after he left Britain in AD 84 or 85. This attribution of so much to Agricola, including responsibility for the creation of Dere Street, is one facet of the abundant loose talk and woolly thinking about Roman roads which is discussed in Chapter 6.

At this stage it may be worth recapping on what has been learned about the planning of Roman roads from this study of Dere Street. It should be remembered that Dere Street may not have been regarded by the Romans as a single road. The long-distance planning seems to have been carried out by at least three different teams of surveyors, working in different directions, whilst the planning and construction of the deviations appear to have been quite piecemeal in both place and timing, and therefore were probably dependant upon the availability and skills of the troops at the time. Hence the planning of Dere Street is likely to have been quite representative of a wide range of Roman road planning tactics in that era.

From this study, it appears that, typically, but not invariably, the Romans:

a) began by setting out a framework of long-distance alignments that established the broad direction that their road was to follow;

b) they then set out deviations from this framework to achieve local objectives, such as avoiding flood plains or accessing suitable river crossings, or detouring to service a newly established fort or town;

c) the planning of these deviations could sometimes be in the opposite directions to that of the long distance frameworks; the choice appears to have been entirely dictated by local circumstances;

d) the deviations seem likely, in the main, to have been set out at the time of construction, and by surveyors with lesser skills than those who set out the long-distance alignments;

e) there may have been a substantial gap in time (several years, in places) between the setting out of the long-distance alignments and the planning of the deviations;

f) where a change of direction took place, on both long-distance alignments and deviations, the minimum angle of change appears to have been about 2 or 3 degrees; it is possible that this may reflect some limitation in the Romans' instrumentation – although this is simply speculation on my part.

Before leaving Dere Street, there is one final point to be made that could warrant further study.

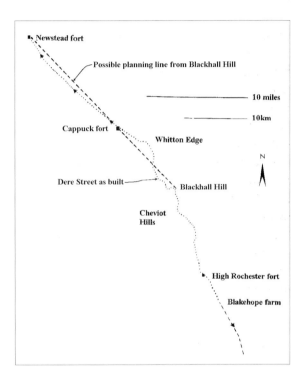

Figure 25: Position of Cappuck fort on a possible long-distance planning line between Blackhall Hill and Newstead fort.

In its passage northwards through the Cheviot Hills, Dere Street breasts the shoulder of Blackhall Hill, and from this point the Roman soldiers (and surveyors) would have had their first view of the fort of Newstead, 20 miles (32km) away to the north, below the Eildon Hills. See Figure 25. Blackhall Hill would have been a natural point from which to set out a long-distance planning alignment to Newstead, and although I could find no evidence that the Romans did create or make use of an alignment from there, it is noteworthy that the fort at Cappuck, located between the Cheviot Hills and Newstead, is almost exactly located on what would have been such a line, had it existed.

If this had been the sole example, it could easily be dismissed as pure coincidence. However, the fort at Ebchester lies exactly on the long-distance alignment from Esh to the Dry Burn, and the fort at Piercebridge lies exactly upon the alignment from

Scotch Corner to Esh. See Figures 20, 21 and 22. Moreover, from the latest excavation reports,[11] the fort at Piercebridge appears not to have been established until the third century. This leads me to wonder if the long-distance alignments may have been more to the Roman administration than simply devices for laying out the courses of roads. As indicated in Chapter 2, it is possible that they may have been connected with the large-scale partitioning of the countryside for administration and control.

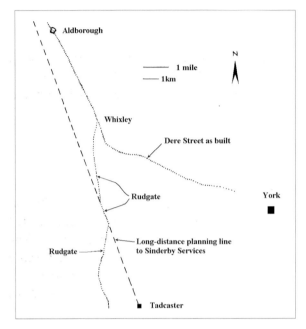

Figure 26: Use of part of the long-distance planning line for Dere Street by the Rudgate Roman road.

Certainly the planning line from Tadcaster to Sinderby Services appears to have served more than one purpose. At some time after the deviation from Dishforth to York had been built via Aldborough, another Roman road, nowadays called the Rudgate, appears to have been built from a point on this deviation at Whixley. From there it pursued a rather zig-zag course in a southerly direction that eventually linked into the Roman road network to the south and west of Tadcaster. See Figure 26. Along its way north of Tadcaster, the Rudgate can be seen to fall on to and follow the planning line from Tadcaster to Sinderby Services for about 1 mile (1.6km). It therefore appears that this planning line would still have been marked out on the ground, even after the course of Dere Street had been constructed elsewhere. This seems to strengthen my suspicion that there may have been multiple purposes for these long-distance alignments, and that this could therefore be a subject worthy of further investigation.

---

11 Cool and Mason 2008, 311; see also Bidwell and Hodgson, 2009, 147-8.

FINDINGS FROM OTHER ROMAN ROADS

Even when Roman roads appear not to have been set out using long-distance alignments, and thus their directions of planning cannot be diagnosed – at least by my methodology – it can still be possible at times to deduce some informative features about their planning from studies of their lines.

EXAMPLE OF AN UNALIGNED ROMAN ROAD

The so-called Stanegate Roman road is an example of an unaligned Roman road – except perhaps at its western end where, as mentioned in Chapter 1, I have a suspicion that it may have been built under a different command. The Stanegate is believed to have run from Corbridge on the River Tyne to Carlisle on the River Eden, although in fact its course is not known at the eastern end, once away from Corbridge, and its final approach to Carlisle remains unknown too. See Figure 27.

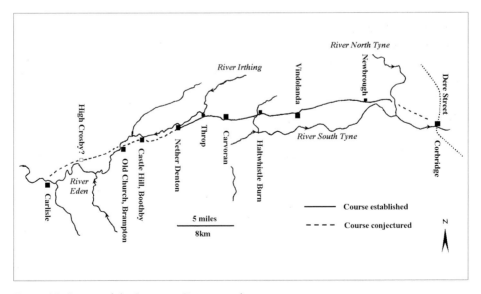

Figure 27: Course of the Stanegate Roman road.

Its route has been established from Warden Hill, west of the River North Tyne, from which point it runs fairly directly past the Roman forts and fortlets at Newbrough, Vindolanda (Chesterholme), Haltwhistle Burn, Carvoran and Throp. Past Throp, it seems (unlike Hadrian's Wall) not to have crossed the River Irthing near Willowford but to have adopted a curving course staying along the lower slopes of the land on the south side of the Irthing. As such, it runs past the fort at Nether Denton and the fort or fortlet at Castle Hill, Boothby, before seemingly taking a straighter line across the Irthing near Irthington and then heading for Crosby and on towards Carlisle. In short, its course is far from confirmed in many places, but enough of it exists for some conclusions to be drawn from the line that it takes.[1]

It used to be supposed that the Stanegate had been planned (by Agricola, again) as a link between the main Roman roads to the north up the eastern and western sides of the Pennine Hills. See Figure 1. It was thought that forts had then gradually become established along its line at Corbridge, Vindolanda, Carvoran and Nether Denton (and possibly close by, at Old Church, Brampton), starting at the time when, following Agricola's departure from Britain, the Romans had decided to withdraw from northern Scotland and fall back to, amongst other strategic positions, the Tyne – Solway line, around AD 86. It was further believed that towards the end of this process, fortlets, including those at Haltwhistle Burn and Throp, were added to this line during Trajanic or even early Hadrianic times. It was envisaged that this would have been to strengthen the link and possibly to help to convert it into an embryonic frontier before Hadrian himself arrived on the scene and decided to build his Wall.[2]

Yet if you remove the forts and fortlets from the line of the Stanegate, you can see that parts of its course would be nonsensical. Starting with a clean sheet, as it were, over the landscape, no one would set out a road between Corbridge and Carlisle on the line that the Stanegate appears to take, which is riddled with unnecessary curving lines, steep inclines and declines, and awkward stream and river crossings. Fortunately, this is not just a hypothetical observation: it can be compared with practical alternatives. The Military Road which was built between Newcastle and Carlisle in 1761-5, following the 1745 Jacobite uprising, adopts a much more direct route over the same ground. Moreover, even though it does possess some very steep sections it is in general far less undulating than the Stanegate. Even the Newcastle to Carlisle Railway, which runs between the Military Road and the Stanegate to the south of the River Irthing pursues a much more level route there without much recourse to substantial cuttings and embankments.

From its line, therefore, there appears to be little doubt that the Stanegate road was neither laid out nor built before the positions of not just the forts but also the

---

1   Poulter 1998.

2   See Breeze 2006, 26-7 and 49-50 for a more detailed account of these developments.

fortlets had been decided by the Roman military authorities. Excavations of the fortlets have shown that they were likely to have been founded in Trajanic or early Hadrianic times.[3] Hence the Stanegate too is most likely to have been the creation of Trajanic or even early Hadrianic times, not Agricolan. This is something that the line of the Stanegate spells out, even though it is a line that appears to have been planned without long-distance alignments. Indeed, the absence of long-distance alignments would appear to support this interpretation of its creation. Long-distance alignments would not have been helpful in setting out the course of the Stanegate if its purpose had simply been to link up the chain of forts and fortlets that had already been established or planned.[4]

THE DISAPPEARANCE OF ROMAN ROADS

The fact that so many stretches of the Stanegate have not been found, despite extensive searches on the ground and from the air, is not uncommon. Many Roman roads seem to disappear for some distances, and then re-appear – often on exactly the same alignment. Plate 1 offers an example of this for the western main Roman road into northern Britain. Yet it is not just that such roads can disappear from view: digging for them can sometimes reveal nothing in the ground between the known stretches too.

The possible reasons for such disappearances have often attracted my attention: what might have been the various factors at work, I wondered, that would cause a stretch of road to survive intact in one place and yet have been obliterated in another? However, with so much undocumented activity that has taken place in our countryside since the Romans left, I doubted that I would ever be able to detect what these factors might have been.

And then it occurred to me: the same factors could be at work in our own era, in connection with the disappearance of railway lines, of which there has been an abundance in Britain since the time of Dr Beeching. From my observations, abandoned railway lines seemed to be disappearing in very similar ways to Roman roads. In some places the track formation would remain as clear as when the rails were last lifted, whereas in others all trace of the line would have been removed, leaving no indication at all that a railway had ever been there. Moreover, all this had been happening over the last forty to fifty years. Hence I had the opportunity to examine such factors at work, and to ask people who had seen what had happened in specific locations to describe to me what changes had taken place, and what the causes had been.

---

3   A Trajanic date for the fortlets appears more likely, because changes made to the fortlet at Haltwhistle Burn suggest a longer period of occupation than an early Hadrianic date would allow (David Breeze pers. comm.).

4   A more detailed account of this analysis is given in Chapter 10, where it is used to illustrate a process for the interpretation of archaeological data.

Thus, although it might appear an unconventional analogy to take, I set out to study the disappearance of an abandoned railway, and the line that I chose was the former Midland Counties Railway line from Rugby to Leicester – or, strictly, to Wigston North Junction, just south of Leicester.[5] At one stage this had been part of the main railway line from London to the midlands, the north-east, and even Scotland for a short while. Hence it had been built as a main line, with substantial embankments and cuttings across decidedly undulating countryside. To my mind, it wasn't going to disappear casually, without the impact of the kinds of major factors that I hoped to investigate. Moreover, to a large extent it had not been artificially preserved as a cycle track or recreational routeway.

As it happens, the line had been abandoned in 1962, somewhat before Dr Beeching's cuts, and I first surveyed its remains some 30 years afterwards, in 1992. I followed this up with a re-survey some ten years later, to see what night have changed over the intervening years. In the process I examined the entire 16½ miles (26.6km) of the abandoned line on the ground and from aerial photographs.

By 2004, some 74 per cent of the original trackbed remained intact, though often overgrown, and pressed into service for new uses, such as:

- a convenient facility for dog walking and taking short cuts near villages;
- a nature reserve;
- a plantation for growing Christmas trees;
- for fly tipping (i.e. illicit dumping of refuse);
- and reservation as a test track for pneumatic tyres – although eventually it was not put to that use.

Perhaps surprisingly, only 1.5 per cent of the line had simply been returned to agriculture directly. Of the remaining 24.5 per cent of the line, this had variously been removed or built over for a variety of reasons, including:

- filling up a cutting that had become used as an impromptu rubbish dump by a nearby housing estate;
- as a site for new industrial estates and a housing development in one of the villages;
- as a landfill site (official rubbish dump) by a county council, after which it had been returned to agriculture, but fitted with vents for methane emissions;
- obliteration by motorways and new road crossings.

---

5   Poulter 2005.

The foregoing might appear to be a rather rum collection of non-Roman activities, but in fact it is quite easy to abstract general principles from their occurrence. These general principles are, I believe, that:

a) the physical remains would be left intact until somebody found a use for them or for the land that they occupied;

b) the timing, location and nature of such re-use was likely to be sporadic and entirely dependent upon local circumstances, and could not be predicted from any direct connection with or relationship to the original purpose of the railway.

These conclusions – simple and almost obvious in themselves – would, I believe, be valid not just for abandoned railways but for any linear legacies such as Roman roads. What was striking about the removal of the railway line was that when it did occur it usually resulted in the complete destruction of the remains, not just a modification or reduction of their form. This may help, in places, to explain the complete disappearance of Roman roads in certain locations. What I observed that did remain, however, even after the most complete obliteration, was some remnant of the original *line* of the railway, either in the form of a fence, a wall, or a property boundary. It appeared that in this respect the legal framework of land tenure would outlast the physical disappearance of the remains.

This is a characteristic that appears to apply to Roman roads too. Quite often their lines seem to be preserved only in the forms of hedgerows and parish boundaries. For comparison, therefore, I took the line of the Roman road known as Akeman Street from Alchester near Bicester to Cirencester, as marked on the Ordnance Survey maps. This road runs through well farmed countryside not dissimilar to that between Rugby and Leicester, but some 30 miles (48km) or more to the south of it. I found that physically there is almost nothing to be seen nowadays of the original Roman remains of this road along any of its line, and yet 78 per cent of its length of 35 miles (c.56km) was still (as at 2004) represented by either modern roads, farm tracks, or field or parish boundaries. After up to 1600 years of neglect and partial disuse (as a through road), and potentially many opportunities for revisions of land tenure through Anglo-Saxon, Norman, Medieval, and post-Medieval times, this survival of so much of the original line of this stretch of Roman road seems quite remarkable, and does indeed seem to support the impression that the legal existence of the line is likely to outlast the physical survival of the remains.

ROMAN SKEW BRIDGES?

There are several instances shown on maps where Roman roads appear to have crossed rivers on the skew, i.e. not at right angles to the flow. Along Dere Street, for instance, the line of the Roman road appears to have crossed the Jed Water at Jedfoot, the River Rede near Elishaw (see Figure 28), and the River Wear opposite Binchester (see Figure 21) on the skew, and the piers of the bridge at Corbridge, which can still be inspected under the water, certainly take a course aslant the flow of the modern River Tyne. Such instances are usually explained on the basis that the courses of the rivers will have changed since Roman times, and that the Romans had no knowledge of the skew arch. Certainly Colin O'Connor's listing and descriptions of all known bridges in the Roman empire appears to include no evidence that the Romans had developed the geometrical construction required to construct a stone or brick arch on the skew.[6]

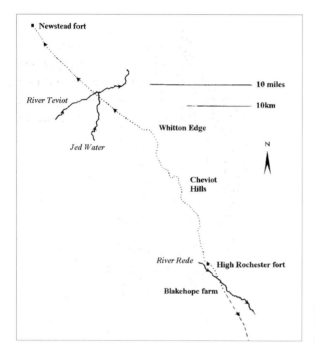

Figure 28: Possible crossings by Dere Street of the Jed Water and the River Rede on the skew.

If a masonry arch is to be constructed on the skew, then unless the angle of skew is very slight, the arch will tend to shear when loaded. The invention of the skew arch succeeded in spreading the load by adopting winding courses of masonry, and it seems to have been something that can be credited in the British Isles to canal engineers at the end of the eighteenth century. From then on it was used extensively by canal and railway engineers to carry their lines over and under existing roads and rivers at other than right angles, so enabling them to avoid undesirable zig-zags in the flow of the traffic or the water.[7]

---

6   O'Connor

7   Boucher 1963, 46-8, although he is probably incorrect in claiming that the invention of the skew arch can be attributed to John Rennie.

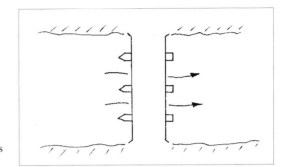

Figure 29: Plan view of the standard Roman masonry bridge at right angles to the flow of the water.

Thus, as far as I know, all Roman masonry bridges which had piers in the water crossed the flow at right angles. See Figure 29. Technically, it is possible to have a line of piers laid out at an angle across the flow of a river, and then to span the piers with timber beams, so as to create a bridge that does cross the stream on the skew, but I do not know of any example where the Romans did this. See Figure 30.

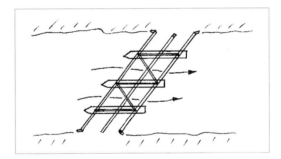

Figure 30: Plan view of a hypothetical skew bridge with beams set on piers staggered across the flow of the water.

However, there is one form of bridge construction used by the Romans which would have allowed waterways to be crossed at other than a right angle, and that is of simple wooden bridges standing on posts driven into the river bed. See Figure 31.

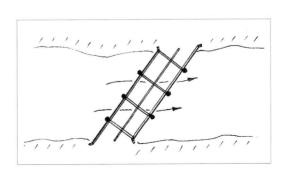

Figure 31: Plan view of a skew bridge with beams set on posts driven into the bed of the stream.

Figure 32: Possible appearance of a Roman bridge carrying Dere Street over Hunwick Gill. (*Illustration reproduced by kind permission of the Archaeological Journal and the Royal Archaeological Institute*)

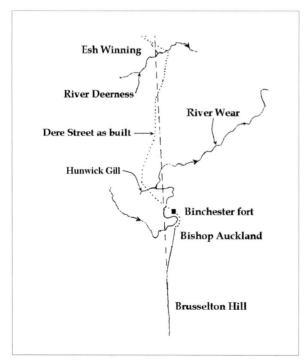

Figure 33: Map showing the location of Hunwick Gill.

It appears that timber bridges like this would have been the normal form of bridge construction for the Romans in Britain, and that the large monumental stone bridges carrying Dere Street over the River Tees and the River Tyne, and Hadrian's Wall over the North Tyne, were exceptions to general practice.[8] The posts of a simple wooden bridge driven into the river bed would not need to have been set in line with the flow, so that if it had been desired, constructing the bridge on the skew would not have been difficult. An artist's impression of such a bridge was published by the *Archaeological Journal* in 1961, and it seeks to show Dere Street crossing Hunwick Gill, on the western side of the River Wear, above Binchester.[9] See Figures 32 and 33. As it happens, the illustration shows the bridge slightly on the skew to the stream, but there is no proof that this was actually the case in Roman times.

To conclude, therefore: it is possible that the Romans were able to set out their roads to cross some rivers and streams on the skew. However, since it is difficult for us to determine what might have been the precise direction of flow of rivers and streams in Roman times, whether or not they ever did so may be something that we will never know for certain.

8   Bidwell and Holbrook 1989, 138.
9   Dymond 1961, plate VIIIB, facing page 139.

6

LOOSE TALK AND
WOOLLY THINKING

There is certainly room for more research to be undertaken on Roman roads in Britain, and some of the questions that might be addressed are discussed in Chapter 8. In the meantime there is much amongst past and recent writings that needs to be redressed.

The most comprehensive source of information about the coverage of the Roman road network in Britain remains I. D. Margary's *Roman Roads in Britain*, first published in 1955.[1] In this he describes the course of every road believed at the time to have been Roman, and gives references to the archaeological investigations carried out on them. His system of numbering the roads (for example, he refers to various stretches of Dere Street as 8a, 8b, 8c, 8d, 8e, etc.) is used as the standard reference to them in archaeological reports to this day, e.g. Margary 8d, for the stretch of Dere Street from Binchester to Corbridge.

Subsequent work has added to the network described by Margary. E. Waddelove has reported a whole network of roads in North Wales, through a lifetime of fieldwork,[2] whilst other researchers such as Martin Allan have devoted an entire book to recording the course of a single road – in his case a road from Brougham near Penrith through the Whinlatter Pass in the Lake District to Moresby on the Cumberland coast.[3] In addition, *Britannia*, published by the Society for the Promotion of Roman Studies, contains brief reports each year of the findings of possible Roman roads that had been encountered by its correspondents in the preceding few months.

The trouble with much research on Roman roads in Britain, especially in the past, is that it has suffered from too much enthusiasm and too little scholarship, as a result of which loose thinking has abounded. The example has already been cited in which the course of Dere Street as it descends from the Cheviot Hills towards Newstead is often described as being aligned upon the Eildon Hills. This ignores the fact that there are three Eildon Hills, and they run north-east to south-west, not to the north-west like the Roman road, so that Dere Street could not have been aligned

---

1   The third edition was published in 1973; see Margary 1973.

2   Waddelove 1999.

3   Allan 1994.

upon all three of them at the same time. Furthermore, as already indicated, careful inspection reveals that little if any part of Dere Street appears to have been aligned upon any particular point on these hills during its descent from Whitton Edge.

Similarly, the attribution of much of the Roman road network in northern Britain to Agricola is simply sloppy thinking. Even if some of the roads had been planned or built during his time as governor, he is unlikely to have had anything to do with them personally. Looking ahead, but in a similar vein, a recent book purporting to be a serious account of the history of Hadrian's Wall would have us believe that Hadrian jumped on a horse in Newcastle and rode across to Carlisle pointing out where his Wall should go. As we shall see, the line of Hadrian's Wall was planned much more carefully than that. Indeed, attributing such actions to known personalities from the past, and dramatising them like film stars, discredits the considerable organisational and technical skills and abilities of the Roman administration and army.

In the 1950s, a group of individuals, enthused by the work that Margary had been doing, began calling themselves the *Viatores* and became convinced that they had discovered a dense network of Roman roads in the English home counties. Every sequence of hedgerows or bumps in a field which looked as if they might be in some sort of alignment was taken to be a trace of a Roman road.[4] I inspected some of their claims on the ground and soon became disillusioned by what I felt was misinterpretation of the evidence. However, it was the Conservation Section of Bedfordshire County Council, faced with the need to produce an account of Bedfordshire in the Roman period, that did what the *Viatores* should have done. They checked the publicly available historic maps, especially the enclosure maps and award books of the late eighteenth and nineteenth centuries, and showed that nearly all of the apparent straight alignments had nothing to do with the Romans. The result was graphically illustrated in the publication of this work, by Angela Simco and her team, in 1984 and it is reproduced here as Figures 34 to 37.[5] As can be seen, virtually all of the *Viatores'* claimed Roman roads in Bedfordshire were wiped off the map.

Where the *Viatores* had gone wrong was in reversing the use of evidence for descriptive purposes that had been adopted by Margary. Even when a Roman road has been proven by excavation or strongly suggested by aerial photography, quite often the only indications of its course to be seen by the observer on the ground are lines of hedgerows and occasionally a ridge running through fields. This was how Margary described many of the roads in his nationwide survey. After all, one of his aims had been to describe the courses of the roads where visible on the ground. But to reverse the process – to proceed from a description to a sole deduction – is fallacious. There are many reasons other than the existence of

---

4   *Viatores* 1964.

5   Simco 1984, 79. The maps were produced by Angela Simco and the Conservation Section of Bedfordshire County Council and are reproduced by courtesy of Central Bedfordshire Council and Bedford Borough Council.

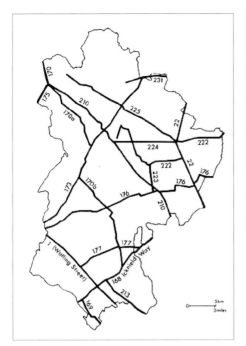

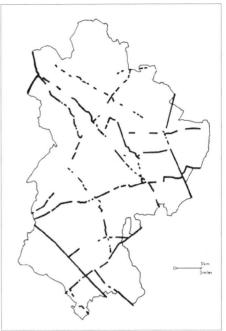

Figure 34: The network of Roman roads in Bedfordshire as proposed by the *Viatores.*

Figure 35: The evidence claimed by the *Viatores.*

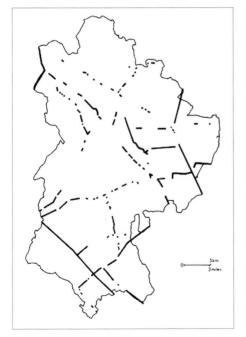

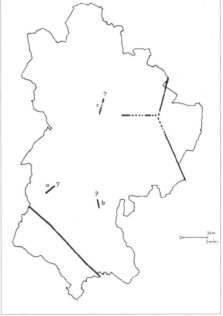

Figure 36: The claimed evidence after removal of modern features.

Figure 37: Remains of the network after removal of the features which show little sign of Roman engineering.

(Maps reproduced by courtesy of Central Bedfordshire Council and Bedford Borough Council)

Roman roads for lines of hedgerows and bumps in fields that happen to be more or less in alignment, and the *Viatores* failed to take account of these alternatives when jumping to their conclusions. Their failure was in the interpretive process, which is a subject that I will attempt to address in Chapter 10.

Although it is not strictly related to Roman roads, an even more spectacular example of flawed analysis is offered by Alfred Watkins's book *The Old Straight Track*.[6] In the early 1920s, Watkins became seized by the idea that prehistoric peoples in Britain had marked out extensive lengths of dead straight alignments over the countryside, in order to help travellers navigate their ways across it. He called these alignments ley lines. A revolutionary concept, Watkins took a true revolutionary's approach to demonstrating it, absorbing and presenting any evidence of whatever kind that might appear to support his case, and ignoring all evidence of any kind that might contradict it. To bolster his case, he even drafted in support from the then recently discovered tomb of Tutankhamun in Egypt. His analysis was so unbalanced and selective in its use of evidence that it could almost be guaranteed to be wrong. As it happens, a professional archaeologist, Tom Williamson, and a colleague, Liz Bellamy, have systematically examined all of the assumptions upon which Watkins's claims were based, and showed that all of them were unfounded.[7] Hence any lurking notions amongst the serious archaeological community that there might just be something in Watkins's idea could be dismissed.

Another individual who, it appears, could be seized by an idea and then be blind to every alternative possibility was the late Raymond Selkirk. Perceptively, he appears to have recognised that the course of Dere Street from the Dry Burn to Beukley was exactly aligned upon the Roman fort at Ebchester, and concluded therefore that the line of Dere Street that turned at Beukley to cross the River Tyne at Corbridge and then returned to the original line at Ebchester must have been a deviation. As discussed in Chapter 4, I agree with him on the latter point, but it appears that he then jumped to the conclusion that the original line of Dere Street must have been not just planned but built between Ebchester and Beukley.

This line crosses the River Tyne near Bywell, and Selkirk's assumption apparently led him to excavate just north of that crossing point to look for evidence of what he called 'Proto Dere Street'. See Figure 38. He claims to have found such evidence,[8] but a photograph that he reproduces of a culvert under the road appears to show the surface covered by slabs of much more modern appearance, strongly suggesting that what he had found was not Roman. He also reported other indications of his postulated Proto Dere Street further north, between Bywell and Beukley.[9] I traced some of these on the ground, and found myself unconvinced, to put it mildly. It

---

6   Watkins 1972.

7   Williamson and Bellamy 1983.

8   Selkirk 1995, 103.

9   Selkirk 1995, 104-5.

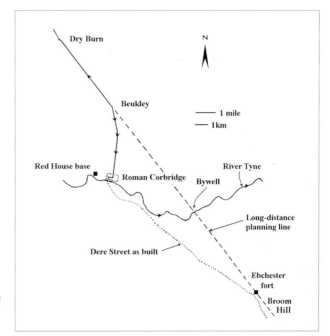

Figure 38: The long-distance planning line crossing the River Tyne near Bywell.

appears that the mistake that Selkirk made was to misunderstand Roman planning processes. In particular, it seems he failed to understand that deviations such as that down to Corbridge are likely to have been laid out only at the same time that construction was – at long last – taking place. Hence it is unlikely that a direct line for Dere Street between Ebchester and Beukley had ever been built.

On the other hand, whenever people do find the remains of an old solidly built road in Britain, there is nearly always a tendency for them to attribute its construction to the Romans. Hugh Davies describes two instances where people have come unstuck on such assumptions. The first occurred in the Forest of Dean, when a notably well and neatly built stone road was discovered. Doubtless, on these grounds it was immediately ascribed to be Roman, despite the facts that it was far narrower than normal Roman roads and conspicuously curved. The falsity of this claim was demonstrated only recently, when excavation under the road exposed charcoal from an Anglo-Saxon bonfire.[10]

The more famous example is that of the road over Blackstone Edge, north-east of Manchester. See Plate 14. Even authorities such as Margary were wont to acclaim this stretch of pavement as one of the finest surviving remains of a Roman road anywhere in Britain. This was unprofessionally lax language on their parts, because even if the road had been Roman its construction was quite unlike that of any other Roman road of which I am aware, and it certainly could not be cited as

---

10 Davies 2002, 28-9.

a typical example of such. As it happens, recent work by the Greater Manchester Archaeological Unit has shown that the road is likely to have been constructed in the eighteenth century, and that the unusual groove down the middle of the road is probably the result of some form of cable operation to assist the transport of wagons up and down the steep 1 in 4 (c.25 per cent) slope.[11]

Even when an old road or track is not well built, or shows little sign of construction at all, some writers can still describe them as Roman, sheltering behind the claim that the Romans would have used the route anyway. It is easy to forget how long the Romans occupied Britain. Except in Scotland, it was for 300 years or more. From today, that would take us back to the time of Queen Anne, or even earlier. It is therefore highly likely that in their time Roman feet will have trodden wherever we can tread now. But that is not the same as stating that the Romans built roads everywhere. In Britain it appears that the Romans made their considerable investment in the building and maintenance of their roads for the purposes of controlling and administering their conquered territory, rather than for the convenience of their citizens. Therefore, although Roman roads continue to be discovered in this country, it is likely that further research will tend to confirm that they were concentrated upon linking towns, forts, and ports, and to be more akin in their coverage to our modern motorway and trunk road network than to the dense fabric of B and C roads with which our countryside is criss-crossed nowadays. Undoubtedly there will have been a dense network of local tracks in Roman times. Many of them would probably have been in existence before the Romans arrived, and have continued in use afterwards. But, away from the towns and forts, carefully aligned and solidly built roads for marching troops and supplies are likely to have been a considerably less common feature of the landscape than that manifested by our modern road network.

From my own observations, Roman roads may even have been less common than is generally credited today. Across the hills in northern Britain there are a number of well-built roads which run fairly directly across the landscape but which are now derelict. These can easily fool the unwary or the inexperienced into thinking that they might have found a Roman road. They certainly fooled me when I began looking for Roman roads in the north.

So what are the features that might enable a later road to be distinguished from a Roman one? In general, the later roads have sharper profiles than Roman roads: their edges are more crisply cut, and their surfaces are flatter, smoother, and less overgrown – reflecting the fact that they may be only 200 or 300 years old rather than 1600. Roman roads, on the other hand, tend to be more rounded in profile, and lumpier and rougher and more ragged at their edges, and after so many years of neglect and abandonment can look as if they are a natural part of the landscape. On one of my early sorties, looking for the western main Roman road to the north as it descended from the fells above Tatham and Bentham in West Yorkshire, I was

11 Davies 2002, 28-9, 81-3.

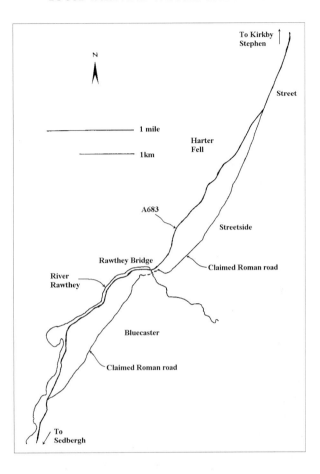

Figure 39: Doubtful Roman road between Sedbergh and Kirkby Stephen.

surprised not to be able to find it. The course was clearly marked on the Ordnance Survey map, and I checked my map-reading again and again to see where I might have gone wrong. It was only after several minutes that I realised I was standing on the road! What I had thought was a natural rise in the ground had become so much part of the landscape that I had failed to recognise it as artificial.

Based upon my observations on the ground, there are a number of roads in the north of England which are reportedly Roman and which are included in Margary's book, but about which I am sceptical.

Sedbergh to Kirkby Stephen (Margary 731): this is a surprisingly direct road which runs north-northeastwards beside a hill called Bluecaster and then between Harter Fell and Ravenstonedale Common towards Kirkby Stephen, passing places such as Streetside and Street Farm along the way. Despite these names, which are suggestive of an old road, I am doubtful that the remains that are visible nowadays are those of a Roman road. See Figure 39. The northernmost 2 miles (3.2km) of this road, down to Rawthey Bridge are tar macadamised, although very narrow. South of Rawthey Bridge the road takes a cleverly engineered route beside Bluecaster Side that runs just along the shelf where the streams falling from Bluecaster down to the

River Rawthey begin to break into ravines. These ravines have to be crossed at a much lower level by the later main road (the A683) which runs nearer the Rawthey and which may have been designed on the principle of a ruling gradient so as to even out the descent. The earlier road certainly seems to have been well planned, but the derelict course beside Bluecaster looks much too modern to be Roman, and I suspect that it will simply have been a predecessor to the later A683.

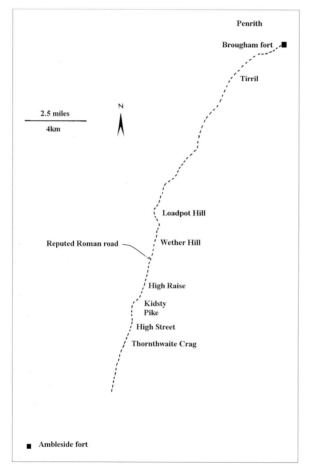

Figure 40: Reputed Roman road over High Street between the forts at Brougham near Penrith and, presumably, Ambleside.

High Street, from Penrith to Troutbeck, east of Ambleside (Margary 74): I had followed this road on the ground, and where I could observe indications of its course I found the line plotted on the Ordnance Survey's 1 inch to 1 mile Tourist Map of the Lake District to be very accurate. See Figure 40. In amongst all the walkers' tracks, there certainly seemed to have been an old road up there too on the high ground, and it appeared to have been well built in places, but the construction didn't look to me to be typical of a Roman road. Nevertheless I accepted the general verdict that the road was Roman until Tom Clare, when

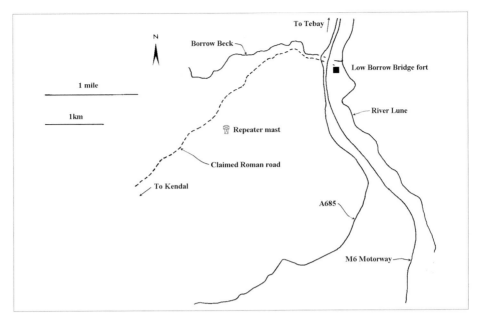

Figure 41: Doubtful Roman road between Low Borrow Bridge fort and Kendal.

County Archaeologist for Westmorland, put the question to me: do you think it *is* Roman? After much reflection, based upon what I have seen, I am now inclined to doubt that this road is of Roman construction.[12]

Low Borrow Bridge to Kendal (Margary 707): this road is described briefly by Margary but at greater length and in more detail by Philip Graystone in his book *Walking Roman roads in Lonsdale and the Eden Valley*.[13] See Figure 41. Although derelict in places, the course of the road is quite easy to follow from Low Borrow Bridge up to the point where it becomes surfaced in concrete to provide access from the Kendal direction to the modern telecommunications repeater mast at the summit below Whinfell Common. However, the remains appear to be generally non-Roman in character and far too crisply cut to be really ancient. In fact the only short stretch of road which does have a Roman profile appears to lie on top of the more crisply cut road. There can be little doubt that there would have been frequent (possibly daily) contact between the Roman forts at Low Borrow Bridge and Watercrook, near Kendal, in those periods when both forts had been in commission at the same time, and that the natural route to have taken between

---

12 The published references cited by Margary for this road reveal surprisingly slight evidence of Roman construction. Complementing my own impressions, T. Hay (one of Margary's references) observes that what is far more noticeable than the presence of metalling in certain places is its total absence in many others.

13 Graystone 2002, 50-4.

them would have followed the line of this road, but if the Romans had indeed built a road here its remains do not appear to me to be visible today.

Apart from my own doubts, fieldwork elsewhere has sometimes eliminated perceived Roman roads from the record. The well-known *Doctor's Gate* road (Margary 711) from Brough-on-Noe to Glossop in North Derbyshire has now been shown to be a post-Medieval diversion, possibly from a genuinely Roman road running approximately 1½ miles (2.4km) to the south.[14]

Whilst this Chapter up to now may have expressed caution about the work of predecessors, it has not meant to imply in any way that those mentioned were frivolous about their contributions to scholarship, even if it is felt that they might have been misguided at times in their approaches or interpretations. However, recently a new form of literature has grown up of which readers who are serious about scholarship need to beware. Usually written by journalists or people connected with the media, books are being published which are purported to be serious accounts of history or archaeological research but which are often no more than thinly disguised scripts for TV documentaries. These days, no one expects a TV documentary to be interested in presenting a wholly complete and accurate picture of the state of research into a specific subject. The number one aim appears to be to present something that will restrain the viewer from switching to another channel. Thus the result is to create something that is relentlessly attention-grabbing, never mind that more than one point of view might be eligible or that several degrees of uncertainty ought to be registered. Such accounts can be very presentable or readable – journalists, after all, are skilled at telling stories – but they often show little real interest in conveying information accurately or in ascertaining the truth about the unknown.

Misinformation, though, is not only confined to the printed page or the TV screen. It can take physical forms, and sometimes this can be accidental. For instance, the well-known Roman road from Ribblehead to Bainbridge in Yorkshire (Margary 73) makes a fine sight as it climbs from Gayle Beck up the slope of Cam Fell. See Figure 42. The fabric of the road appears to be exceptionally well preserved at this point. Yet I understand that this road was turn-piked in the eighteenth century, and that therefore what appears on the surface is comparatively modern, and misleading to people who believe what they are inspecting are surviving Roman remains. Presumably the original Roman road lies under what is visible today.

Recent work on Dere Street, undertaken about ½ mile (1km) north of the fort at High Rochester, has revealed two gravelled surfaces overlying the Roman road there, and both of these were considered to be post-medieval in date.[15] Possibly in view of the continuing importance of Dere Street as a north-south route, the excavators also stated that 'It is likely that repairs have been made to the original

---

14 Hart 1984, 92. For a summary of the results of P. Wroe's extensive fieldwork on Roman roads in North Derbyshire see pages 90-4 of this volume.

15 Hale 2007, 46-50.

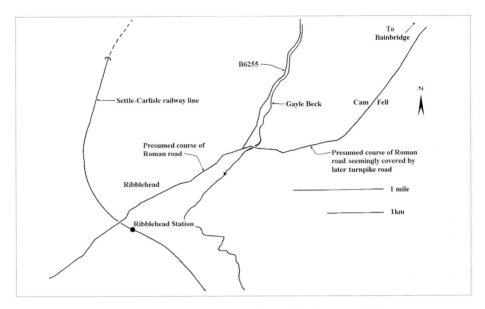

Figure 42: Remains of a Roman road apparently obscured by later resurfacing.

road structure on an *ad hoc* basis ever since Roman times…'. As it happens, both of the later surfaces were found under the modern ground level and were therefore invisible before the excavation. Hence from this and the foregoing we may need to be cautious about assuming that the remains of any Roman road, where visible, may have lain untouched since the Romans departed from Britain.

A slightly different picture may exist on Wheeldale Moor in North Yorkshire (see Plate 15), where the Ministry of Works has exposed to public view about a quarter of a mile of the fabric of what was believed to have been a Roman road. The formation appears to be a very solid mass of densely packed stones set between kerbs, neatly placed so as to maintain a constant width, and with culverts channelled across the stonework at intervals to drain off rainwater. It forms a very impressive exhibit of what the foundation layers of a Roman road may have looked like underneath its final gravelled surface. Unfortunately, it appears that in exposing the remains, the Ministry of Works custodian may have been more than unduly creative in presenting them to public view, and that at least some elements of the appearance today may not be authentically original. Worse than that, it now appears possible that the original remains were not part of a Roman road at all, but the base of a Neolithic boundary bank.[16] If so, the deception, albeit unintended, would have been twofold.

Plates 16 and 17 show a more recent example of such a deception in progress at the site of Portonaccio in Italy. The work may have been undertaken for the sake

---

16 Pete Wilson pers. comm. I am indebted to David Breeze for bringing this uncertainty to my attention.

of appearance rather than as a deliberate act of deception, but once it had been completed many visitors would have left the site thinking that they had walked on a Roman road.

It is a fact, though, that the consolidation of any archaeological remains for the sake of their preservation, and for presentation to public view, is likely to involve a degree of restoration. A good example exists at the site of Roman Corbridge, where quite a large area of the Roman town and military base has been exposed and consolidated for display to the public. There the line of the Stanegate runs prominently across the site from one end to the other and looks very convincing as the course of a typical and much-repaired Roman road through a Roman town. Yet I understand it is in fact a Ministry of Works rebuild. Once the excavations under the road had been carried down to the lowest levels, the upper surfaces would then have been restored for presentation to the public. The rebuild is a very good one, but for those who like to think they are casting their eyes upon authentically Roman remains, it is a rebuild nonetheless.[17] No deception, of course, is intended in such restoration, and it can apply to all consolidated monuments.

Looking ahead to the second half of this book, perhaps the greatest example of consolidation to be found in Britain lies along Hadrian's Wall. Yet some of the magnificently photogenic remains of the Wall that we see today are more than a consolidation: they are a nineteenth-century reconstruction. True, the rebuilding took place on the original Roman foundations, using original stones that had fallen from the Wall as it weathered away, but the key point is that what is visible nowadays is not always what would be seen if nature alone had had its way with the Roman remains.[18] Few of the guidebooks and other publications about the Wall emphasise this fact. There are a small number of places along Hadrian's Wall where the remains are visible but have been neither reconstructed nor consolidated. At Limestone Corner, for instance, those people examining the unfinished state of the Roman ditch there may be unaware that the stony mound on which they are standing is in fact the remains of Hadrian's Wall. Another example of unrestored Wall can be seen much further to the west, near Garthside, between the villages of Banks and Walton (see Plate 25).

To conclude, and looking back over this chapter again, perhaps the overriding impression to be gained from the foregoing is that, as practised by professionals today, archaeology has become a much more rigorous discipline than either amateurs or the general public may appreciate.

---

17 The late Charles Daniels pers. comm. David Breeze (pers. comm.) makes the point that consolidation of any archaeological site entails putting back what has been excavated, so as to make it presentable for viewing by the public. Hence a degree of rebuilding is inevitable in any cultural resource work, and this is what would have happened in the case of the Stanegate after it had been excavated at Corbridge.

18 The consolidation of Hadrian's Wall that was undertaken by the Ministry of Works in the twentieth century entailed no replacement (David Breeze pers. comm.).

COMPARISON WITH THE EIGHTEENTH-CENTURY MILITARY ROADS IN SCOTLAND

As already indicated, Roman roads in Britain appear to have been mainly military roads, and it is instructive to compare them with that other major network of military roads in Britain: the military roads in Scotland. The construction of these was initiated by General (as he later became) Wade in 1725, and was then continued by Major Caulfeild from 1740 to 1767. The early ones especially were built across virgin territory to the disapproval of many of the local population. We may assume that the same would have applied to Roman roads. The countryside of northern Britain may not have been virgin in Roman times, but the Roman planners seem to have treated it as such.

Like the Roman roads in Britain, the military roads in Scotland were primarily intended to support the administration and control of a countryside after conquest – in this case after the suppression of the Jacobite uprising in 1715. There was a conscious secondary aim in that it was hoped that the roads would open up the trade and commerce of the country and thus weaken the tribal structure of society which had contributed so much to the recent uprising. It may be that the creation of Roman roads had a similar subsidiary aim, but we have no record of this.

We are fortunate, however, in having a comprehensive and very scholarly account of the construction of the military roads in Scotland by William Taylor. Not only has he followed them closely on the ground: he has studied the documentation of their creation which is still preserved in the military and Treasury records of the time.[1] Hence we know fairly accurately which roads were built, and when, and we have some picture of the overall costs. We also have access to the correspondence between the road builders and their headquarters and so have insights into the organisation and processes of planning and construction which we so lack with the Roman roads in Britain.

Thus, in Scotland:

- road building did not take place in winter. Under Wade's command, work began on 1 April and ended on the last day of October. Even

---

1 Taylor 1996.

between these limits there were days when work could not be done;

- usually only about half of the work force started in April; the full force were in action only from 1 July;
- in the Highlands the men were either accommodated in huts or tents, that were typically spaced in camps at 10-mile (16km) intervals, but in south-western Scotland the troops were billeted with the civilian population;
- surveying parties under an engineer officer would probably comprise a non-commissioned officer and 6 soldiers;
- the number of men used by Wade to build any one road was usually 500;
- these were divided into working parties, each of 1 captain, 2 subalterns, 2 sergeants, 2 corporals, 1 drummer, and 100 men, together with a small body of from 5 to 11 men as 'reserves' for carrying messages, etc;
- in addition to these men, extensive civilian support was required, including masons, wallers, pavers, carpenters and blacksmiths, and the provision of transport for tools, supplies, and other materials as well as food and drink;
- troops working on the roads were given double pay;
- the work rate was from 1½ to 2 yards (1.4 to 1.8 metres) per man per day;
- in 1731 a workforce of 348 men from April and 510 men from July built the 28 miles (45km) of road over the Corrieyairack Pass from Dalwhinnie to Fort Augustus in a single season, despite being handicapped by almost six weeks of continuous rain. This rate was regarded as an exceptional achievement, however, and at least one of the bridges on the road was not completed until the following year.

We cannot tell how closely these arrangements would have matched those of the Romans, but they give us insights into the logistical factors that the Roman authorities would have had to address when building their own roads.

I find it difficult to estimate the relative efforts required to build Roman roads when compared to the military roads in Scotland. The military roads in Scotland are slightly narrower than a typical Roman road, with a standard width of 16 feet (4.9 m), but William Taylor's book shows them to have had a fairly massive construction, with no less than 2 feet (60cm) or more of gravel as the topmost layer – despite which, regravelling them was an almost annual activity in some places, seemingly because of the severity of the Scottish climate.[2] In contrast, my observations, when following them on the ground, are that the military roads in

---

2   Taylor 1996, 36-7.

Scotland appear to have had a slighter construction than Roman roads and to have become damaged quite rapidly after abandonment. In terms of the effort required for construction, the eighteenth-century soldiers would also, of course, have had the use of gunpowder for blowing up and smashing rocks when making the roads. All told, I am inclined to estimate that it might have taken twice as much effort to build a Roman road than one of the military roads in Scotland over the same distance.

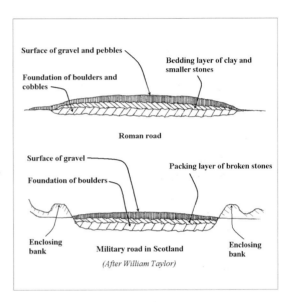

Figure 43: Comparative sections of a Roman road and one of the military roads in Scotland built under General Wade. The comparison is only indicative. There is scarcely any standardisation in the constituents of Roman roads in Britain. Whatever suitable materials were readily to hand seem to have been used. Widths also varied from road to road, typically being from 15 to 22 feet (4.6m to 6.7m), but some of the major Roman roads could be much wider than this. Sometimes Roman roads had ditches running beside them, but this was not always the case.

Figure 43 attempts to show a section through a typical example of each road, drawn to the same scale. A striking characteristic of the military roads in Scotland is the bank which runs on each side of the road. These were formed, and deliberately so, from the material thrown up when excavating the foundation of the road, and at first sight they would appear to have been a handicap to travel. For instance, they would have helped to retain rainwater on the surface of the road, and made it slippery when frozen. When it snowed, they would have ensured that the roadway would have filled up first, and made the going harder, although until the snow reached more than 2 or 3 feet (c.60-90cm) deep, they would at least have made it easier for the traveller to see where the road was located. From William Taylor's illustration, it appears that the main purpose of these roadside banks may have been to stop flood water from getting on to the road. In contrast, the Roman roads were generally cambered so that the water would run off the road. It may be that the unusual feature of the military roads in Scotland is a reflection of the fact that so many of them were built along the sides of mountains in a very wet climate, but this tactic does not seem to have been adopted by later road builders in Scotland.

It is reported that General Wade was impressed by the straightness of Roman roads, and it is possible that he tried to emulate this characteristic in his roads, at least to begin with. It seems highly unlikely, though, that he would have made a study of the planning or construction of Roman roads before embarking on the creation of his own. Therefore he and his team would have had to work out what to do from first principles, and it may be that the unusual profile of his roads was one result of this. Certainly, mistakes were made at first. In 1732, only five years after his earliest road up the Great Glen had been completed from Fort Augustus to Inverness he was having to re-align it to run down to Foyers and follow the side of Loch Ness. This was because the earlier course of the road through Stratherrick had proved difficult to use in winter and in inclement weather.[3] As an indicator of how rapidly roads such as this can disappear, the course of this earlier road is now lost and has become the subject of conjecture.[4]

Despite his apparent admiration of their directness, Wade probably did not understand the style of planning that the Romans applied to their roads. Instead of setting out long-distance alignments and then marking out deviations from them, it appears that Wade's surveyors tended to work on a line-of-sight basis. That is, their roads were planned to run straight as far as the eye could see, but that at the end of the straight, a new direction would be set out, not related to the one that had just been followed, nor to any overall long-distance alignment. An attempt to illustrate this is offered in Plate 18. Taken before the area was covered by forestry, which has now obliterated the view, this photograph shows the line of Wade's road heading from Carn an t-Suide, east of Loch Tarff, towards Whitebridge, between Fort Augustus and Inverness. The annotations on the plate are intended to indicate the differences between the lines taken by Wade's men and those that a Roman surveyor might have followed in this situation.

This line-of-sight style of planning does not represent any weakness of the part of Wade's surveyors. In terms of setting out the best course for a road across a countryside, the Roman practice of marking out very long-distance alignments and returning obdurately to them whenever possible may be considered far less practical than Wade's mode of planning, especially in mountainous landscapes like the Highlands of Scotland.

Nevertheless, Wade's early addiction to straight lines through the Highlands of Scotland became, I think, a source of trouble. This was because it took his roads not only up and down very steep hills but also through bogs and poorly drained moorland. Not only would these latter parts of his roads have been difficult to construct through the morasses: they would also have been expensive to maintain, as they periodically became swamped or sank repeatedly into the bogs. Today,

---

3   Taylor 1996, 45.
4   Taylor 1996, 126; Lawson 2006, 98-9.

from my observations, these are the parts of Wade's roads which can often be the most impassable or obliterated when you try to walk along them.

This point may not have been lost upon Wade's Number two, Major Caulfeild. When he took over the building of the military roads in 1740, the costs of maintenance were already becoming apparent, and we know from the records that over time the Major came under increasing pressure from His Majesty's Treasury to reduce expenses. It is noticeable that the later military roads, built under Caulfeild, although still very direct, have little addiction to being dead straight. Rather, they appear to vary their courses so as to keep to dry ground, and when following them today it is remarkable how many of them remain unsodden underfoot even after abandonment maybe nearly 200 years ago. It is possible that this shift in policy away from complete straightness was the result of the Treasury's pressure on Caulfeild to keep his costs to a minimum.

The interesting point here, though, is that Roman roads, like Wade's earlier ones, did often go straight through marshes and poorly drained land. It is likely that there would have been many more such areas in Roman times than in ours. The conclusion has to be, I think, that compared with the military roads in Scotland, the costs of construction and maintenance of their roads was of little or no concern to the Roman administration. Simply, they had the engineering skills and the manpower to build roads across swamps and marshes and so, when they wanted to, they did. This perhaps illustrates, as much as anything, the importance of their roads to the Romans, and their determination to construct them wherever they considered that they should go. To encapsulate the point, therefore, we may conclude that to the Romans, in the construction of their roads, consideration of the expense appears to have been a secondary matter at best.

8

SOME QUESTIONS FOR
FUTURE RESEARCH

Before departing from Roman roads to explore the planning of Hadrian's Wall, it may be helpful to list some questions that I feel could usefully be addressed in future research on Roman roads.

Firstly, of course, I feel it would be useful to have my methodology applied to Roman roads other than Dere Street, to see what light may be cast upon their planning too. In 2008 I applied it in a fairly casual way to the main western road to the north, from Manchester to Carlisle, as it climbs up Croasdale from the Forest of Bowland. From my observations I formed the clear impression that this stretch of road had been set out from north to south, but I did not pursue my investigation any further than that. No doubt other researchers will be able to advance this work on those Roman roads which interest them. However, before doing so, I would encourage such researchers to study first the *caveats* about the application of the methodology which are given in my full archaeological reports on Dere Street and Hadrian's Wall.[1] It is not difficult to draw wrong conclusions from the methodology if it should be used incautiously.

Secondly, the question of why Roman surveyors should sometimes set out such enormously long planning alignments continues to intrigue. As already suggested, it may be that such planning lines had meant more to the Roman administration than merely being devices for laying out roads. Certainly they do not seem to have been essential to laying out a sensible line for a road, and as far as I am aware neither General Wade nor any of the builders of the turnpike and earlier roads in the seventeenth, eighteenth, and nineteenth centuries in Britain found any need to go to such lengths. Overall, simply for the purpose of determining practical routes for roads, the Roman addiction to setting out long-distance alignments first, and then choosing to stick with them for much of the way, may have been more of a hindrance than a help.

Following on from this, another question which continues to intrigue is why the Romans, having set out deviations from a long-distance planning line, should then so often tend to return to the line rather than head off directly from the deviation to the intended destination. The explanation may be a practical

---

1   Poulter 2009, 6, 22, 35-7.

one. If construction had already started – probably at more than one place along the long-distance line – by the time that it became apparent that a deviation would be required, then the deviation would need to return to the long-distance line to meet up with parts that had already been built. My analysis in Chapter 4 of the course of Dere Street at Leeming may be an example of this. However, other explanations might be possible, and worthy of consideration. For instance, there might have been a division in the Roman command between strategic and tactical planning, with the former taking precedence in the hierarchy and not just in the timing.[2] However, it must be stressed that this is purely speculation on my part.

Finally, the factors that might affect the disappearance of Roman roads have already been discussed in Chapter 5, but more factors might need to be added. For instance, the forces of natural decay would obviously have had a greater effect on a Roman road over 1600 years than they would have had over the dereliction of only forty or fifty years of the abandoned railway line that I used by way of an analogy. Yet, as I discovered, disused railway lines (below the tree line) can very rapidly become overgrown with thorn bushes, wild roses and brambles, and within twenty years or so can be rendered quite impenetrable to any walkers not attired in motorcycle leathers. So can it be assumed that those stretches of Roman roads that have survived in service to this day must have remained in use continually since Roman times? Otherwise, what would have kept them open, or returned them to use?

There may be one or more additional factors at work here, too. Along Dere Street it is noticeable that the parts that have tended to survive into modern times were the long straight or straighter sections, such as from Dishforth to Scotch Corner and on to Bishop Auckland, and from Beukley to the Dry Burn (see Figure 20). Other parts of the course of Dere Street fell out of use over time, and had to be established by fieldwork which was largely carried out in the twentieth century. An example of such is the stretch of Dere Street from the River Deerness towards Ebchester (see Figure 21). Quite often, the stretches that became lost are the less straight portions of the road which seem to me to have been laid out by line-of-sight planning. Might there be, I wonder, some correlation here? This tendency for the straightest parts of Roman roads to survive best seems to me to occur on other Roman roads, and so it suggests to me that there might be one or more general factors at work here, but if so then they have so far been resistant to elucidation on my part.

---

2   Poulter 2009, 24.

CASE STUDY 2, PART 1:
THE PLANNING OF THE LINES OF
HADRIAN'S WALL AND THE VALLUM

My methodology, described in Chapter 3, had been developed in order to determine the direction in which Roman roads might have been set out on the ground, but it was David Breeze and later Nick Hodgson who suggested that I might also try applying it to the planning of Hadrian's Wall. So, after an initial experiment at Limestone Corner,[1] I applied the methodology at first to the eastern sector of Hadrian's Wall, from Newcastle to the crossing of the River North Tyne near Chesters. See Figure 44 on page 80. My observations were made on the ground in 2004 and 2005, and gratifyingly, after analysis, I found that the suggestion appeared to have worked: the methodology gave consistent indications of the direction of planning of Hadrian's Wall from Newcastle all the way to the North Tyne. Moreover, it also appeared to work for the Vallum. The Vallum is the large double bank and ditch that runs behind Hadrian's Wall. However, what the methodology also revealed was that the planning of the line of the Vallum appears to have been quite different from that of Hadrian's Wall.

This study of the eastern sector also revealed, unexpectedly, a feature of the line of Hadrian's Wall that had not, to my knowledge at the time, been reported before, and which seemed to me to cast new light upon what at least one of the purposes of the Wall might have been, and on how it would have worked operationally. Encouraged, I thus extended my study of the Wall and the Vallum all the way from the fort at Chesters on the North Tyne to the western end of the Wall at Bowness-on-Solway. See Figure 44 again. In passing, Plates 19 to 25 show some features of interest along the Wall and the Vallum, and reference is made to these, where apposite, at appropriate junctures in the text.

The observations for this extended study from Chesters to Bowness were mostly undertaken in 2006 and 2007, although the analysis work and further visits to verify some of the observations continued into 2008. There were a few stretches that I had to exclude from this survey of Hadrian's Wall, such as where it runs over the crags from Sewingshields to Walltown, and along the west bank of the River Eden downstream of Carlisle. In these places the Wall does not follow alignments, and so I could not diagnose the direction there in which it might

---

1 Poulter 2008, 99-101.

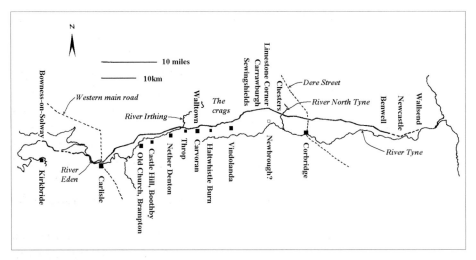

Figure 44: The line of Hadrian's Wall, running from Bowness-on-Solway on the west to Wallsend on the east. Places that are mentioned in the text are shown above the line. Below the line are shown the positions of the forts and fortlets which are believed to have been in commission along the line of the Stanegate Roman road when the course of Hadrian's Wall was being set out.

have been planned. (In contrast, the Vallum does follow alignments along these stretches, and so its directions of planning could be diagnosed throughout by my methodology.)

The results from this extended survey fully matched and confirmed the findings from the eastern sector, for both Hadrian's Wall and the Vallum. However, before proceeding to describe the findings it may be helpful to give a brief description of what the application of my methodology entailed.

As with Dere Street, the fieldwork involved identifying and then visiting every point shown on the map at which Hadrian's Wall and the Vallum changed direction, and then assessing the best field of view at that point. The choice of map was important, because many lengths of the Wall and the Vallum are no longer visible on the ground and therefore the accuracy of the map-making was crucial to my work. The map that I used was the Ordnance Survey Map of Hadrian's Wall, drawn to a scale of 2 inches to 1 mile (1:31,680), and published in 1975.[2] This is a fine tool for archaeological research, and its accuracy has not been seriously undermined by excavations since it was published. Unfortunately it is now out of print, and was replaced in 1989 by the Ordnance Survey's Historical Map & Guide to Hadrian's Wall, which is not suitable for serious research. However, I understand that English Heritage intends to publish a new archaeological map of Hadrian's Wall in 2010, which should help to rectify the situation for the future.

---

2   Ordnance Survey Second edition 1972, updated in 1975.

Taking both surveys together, I calculate that it took me about thirty days in total to make all of my observations along both Hadrian's Wall and the Vallum, but this effort was spread over several visits, and many of the later ones were, as already indicated, to check and double-check my original observations in the light of various possibilities thrown up by my analyses. It was the analyses – making sense of the observations – that took up the major part of my time, as it had done for Dere Street. All told, I think I must have spent about two man-years analysing my observations, making sense of them, and then documenting them in a full archaeological report. This has now been published in the aforementioned BAR monograph 492.[3] Any reader who wishes to examine the full details of my observations and analyses of the directions of planning of Hadrian's Wall and the Vallum is referred to that document.

Before escorting the reader on tours of the planning of the Wall and then the Vallum, it will be helpful, I think, to describe some of the findings that my work has, I believe, uncovered.

The first is that both Hadrian's Wall and the Vallum appear to have been set out using road-planning techniques. When I began work on Hadrian's Wall, although the initial experiment at Limestone Corner had produced positive results, I did not know whether my methodology would work over any extended length of the Wall, and I was pleasantly surprised to find that it did. With hindsight, I think I should have been more surprised than I was, at the time. A designer's objectives when setting out the line of a wall are quite different from those of someone planning a road. Fundamentally, a road is meant to assist passage, whereas a wall is intended to prevent it. Therefore road-planning tactics would seem to be inappropriate ones to use when setting out the line of a wall.

Certainly, one would not expect Roman surveyors to use road-planning tactics when setting out the course of an aqueduct. With an aqueduct, gradient is paramount and directness a poor second. The Romans certainly understood that. It may be that the surveyors who set out the lines of Hadrian's Wall and the Vallum had never done anything like it before. For cross-country work, their main experience may well have lain in setting out roads such as Dere Street, and, if so, this experience is what they may have fallen back upon. As we shall see, by the time that the next generation of Roman surveyors came to set out the Antonine Wall in Scotland, they appear to have profited from the experience gained – but that is for a chapter to come.

Thus it appears that the surveyors who set out the lines of Hadrian's Wall and the Vallum first created, in both cases, a chain of long-distance alignments and then marked out deviations from them to meet local objectives. This appears to have been conducted in just the same way as their predecessors had done along Dere Street, except that the long-distance and deviation-planning activities may well have been parts of the same exercises on these occasions. It was fortunate,

---

3 Poulter 2009, 33-87.

from my point of view, that they did plan the lines in this way because, apart from the aforementioned exceptions where the Wall is unaligned, I was thus able to diagnose their directions of planning from their tactics.

And what emerged from these diagnoses, for both Hadrian's Wall and the Vallum, was completely unexpected, not least by myself. In the past, if pressed, most scholars would probably have ventured a guess that Hadrian's Wall had been laid out by the Romans from east to west, i.e. from Newcastle to Bowness-on-Solway. Intuitively, I think most people would have felt this to have been a more natural thing to do than to have set out the line of the Wall the other way round, from west to east. Even less likely to most people, perhaps, would have been the thought that Hadrian's Wall had been set out from the highest points – the crags – to run down towards the coasts at each end. Instead, what my survey revealed was that what would probably have been considered the least likely option of all had been adopted: the course of Hadrian's Wall appears to have been planned inwards from its eastern and western extremities towards the crags.

In fact, at least five phases of planning can be distinguished:

from the west:

- Bowness-on-Solway to Carlisle;
- from the River Eden to Walltown, at the western end of the crags;

from the east:

- from Newcastle (and possibly Wallsend) to the River North Tyne;
- from the North Tyne to Sewingshields, at the eastern and of the crags;

and then:

- over the crags between Sewingshields and Walltown, direction uncertain.

Even more unexpected was the planning of the Vallum. Except where it runs at the foot of the crags, it appears that it was planned outwards from where each of the forts were (or were to be) located along Hadrian's Wall. It may be worth reminding readers that when Hadrian's Wall was first planned, there were no forts along it. The Wall was simply equipped with a chain of turrets and milecastles spaced along its length at nominally ⅓ Roman mile (539 yards or 493 m) intervals. The forts were added to the Wall after construction had started but apparently before it had been completed.[4] Although archaeologists had long since become convinced that

---

4   Breeze 2006, 51. The fort at Carrawburgh is believed to be an exception, added to the Wall rather later than the others.

the Vallum was constructed after the start of construction of Hadrian's Wall, this new finding ties the Vallum intimately into the decision to place forts along the line of the Wall. From the directions in which it was set out, it appears that the Vallum could not have been planned until the positions of the forts along the Wall had been decided.

It should be noted that neither the directions of planning of Hadrian's Wall nor the Vallum may tell us anything about the directions in which they may have been built. In theory, at least, a line could have been planned from one end and construction started from the other. In practice, I suspect that once the lines had been set out on the ground and the work divided between the legions (and, in the case of the Vallum, between the auxiliary troops),[5] then construction is likely to have started in several places at once, just like on a modern motorway. The evidence appears to support this.[6] In addition, different skills and abilities would have been required to build milecastles and turrets than those required to erect the rampart of the Wall, and they would have been required at different times and in different places in the sequence. For an account of what it may have taken to build Hadrian's Wall (at least in stone – some parts were initially built of turf), and for insights into the logistical processes required, the reader is referred to Peter Hill's recent book on the subject.[7]

The directions of planning are not the only findings that can be deduced from the lines of the Wall and the Vallum. For instance, even if the Vallum had not been planned outwards from the fort sites along the Wall, it is still possible to detect that it was planned after the Wall. There are several places where the line of the Vallum is on collision courses with Hadrian's Wall, but in every case it is the Vallum which turns to avoid the collision, not the Wall.

In fact, there are striking dissimilarities between the lines of Hadrian's Wall and the Vallum, and not just in their directions of planning. The Vallum tends to cut across the countryside in long straight stretches regardless of the topography, rather in the manner of the long-distance alignments of a Roman road. The line of Hadrian's Wall, in contrast, shows considerable concern for the position of the Wall in the landscape, often deviating to high points, seemingly to obtain a better view to the north.

Yet, despite this, what only became apparent slowly in the course of my survey is that the line of the Wall is also carefully chosen to retain, wherever possible, a view to the south. This is something that seems not to have been generally noticed so far, although in his book on *Roman Military Signalling* David Woolliscroft does remark that Hadrian's Wall 'tends to be built along the northern limit of view of

---

5   It appears that the legionaries built the Wall, whereas the auxiliary troops largely constructed the Vallum. This point is discussed further in Chapter 11.

6   David Breeze pers. comm.

7   Hill 2006.

the Stanegate',[8] which it seems to me does amount to the same thing. In fact, this aspect seems to have been a priority for the Wall's designers. In several places, they appear to have sacrificed a good view to the north in order to retain a view to the south. The possible explanations for this behaviour are examined in Chapter 11.

The immediate curiosity, though, is why so few people seem to have remarked on this orientation before. It is not difficult to observe the south-facing aspect of Hadrian's Wall as you travel along it, and thousands of interested and observant people undertake this journey every year. So how is it that this feature has remained largely unnoticed to date? The answer may lie in the old human failing that people only tend to see what they are looking for, and on Hadrian's Wall that is almost always the view to the north – towards where the barbarians were.

There may, however, be a more practical explanation. Without knowing the directions in which the Roman surveyors are likely to have been working, it is harder to grasp what they may have been doing. As soon as you can stand on each point of turn and examine the landscape in the direction in which the Roman surveyors appear to have been looking, you can then assess better the options with which they were faced and the choices that they made. And when you do this, you can see that whilst not neglecting the importance of a view to the north, the Roman surveyors appear to have been giving priority to retaining a view to the south. On this point it is perhaps now timely to pass along the lines of the Wall and then the Vallum to examine in more detail how they appear to have been laid out.[9]

THE PLANNING OF HADRIAN'S WALL

Hadrian's Wall began on the River Tyne at Wallsend, although there is argument about whether or not the Romans' original plan had been to start the Wall further west at Newcastle. This raises the possibility, therefore, that the line eastwards to Wallsend might have been an afterthought.[10] I was not able to diagnose the direction of planning from Wallsend to Newcastle because the area is entirely built up nowadays. Any attempt to determine, in the middle of a housing or an industrial estate, what the best field of view might have been before the area became built up is unlikely to produce dependable results.

At Benwell, however, on the western side of Newcastle, observations of the best fields of view become possible and it appears that Hadrian's Wall was initially

---

8   Woolliscroft 2001, 68.

9   The following accounts of the lines of Hadrian's Wall and the Vallum are necessarily confined to their planning. For a full and up-to-date account of all of the features and structures along the Wall and the Vallum, see the latest *Handbook to the Roman Wall*: Breeze 2006.

10 For a review of the arguments for and against, see Breeze and Hill 2001,1; Hill 2001, 3-18; Bidwell 2003, 17-24.

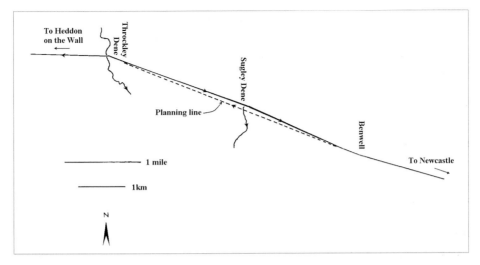

Figure 45: The planning of Hadrian's Wall between Benwell and Throckley Dene.

planned here to head directly from Benwell to Throckley Dene,[11] i.e. from east to west. A dene, by the way, appears to be a local name for a ravine running down to the River Tyne. Notwithstanding this direct line to Throckley Dene, a very slight deviation appears to have been put in to take the Wall around the head of Sugley Dene, which lies in-between, and this deviation appears to have been set out from Throckley Dene back to Benwell, i.e. from west to east. See Figure 45.[12] Thus the initial alignment seems to have served only as a planning line, and the Wall, as built, followed the deviation. This is something that we will see on a number of occasions as we travel along the Wall.

The place where the Roman surveyors chose to take the Wall across Throckley Dene is quite extraordinary, however. Nowadays, it is a substantial ravine more than 200 feet (61 m) across and some 100 feet (30.5 m) deep. It may have been less fearsome in Roman times. Nevertheless it must still have represented a substantial obstacle to be overcome, and it would appear to have called for a significant feat of Roman engineering to convey the Wall across it in such a way that (a) would-be intruders could not steal under it in dry weather and yet (b) the whole structure would not be washed away in a flash flood, to which the Dene looks as if it may once have been prone.

The curious point is that if the Roman surveyors had continued their line from Benwell to Sugley Dene – or possibly had turned a degree or so to the north there – they would have avoided the obstacle altogether. Only about ⅓ mile (c.540 m)

---

11 Formerly known as Walbottle Dene.

12 In all the maps, as with Dere Street, the arrows indicate the diagnosed direction of planning.

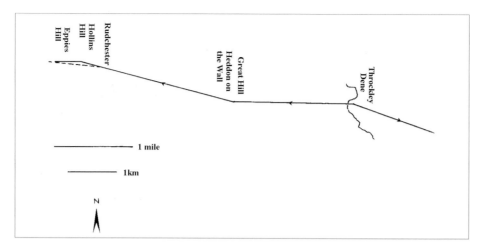

Figure 46: The planning of Hadrian's Wall between Throckley Dene and Rudchester.

north of their chosen crossing-point, the stream feeding into Throckley Dene is only a brook trickling through an almost level meadow. One could easily jump across the stream today, and perhaps more to the point, the Romans could easily have built Hadrian's Wall across it.

The obvious question is why the Roman surveyors should have picked such a difficult spot at which to cross the Dene, and the answer may offer the first example that we have of the Romans' wish to retain a view to the south. On the western side of Throckley Dene, there is a prominent ridge running west-east. If the Romans had crossed Throckley Dene upstream it would have carried the Wall onto the northern slope of this ridge, offering a fair view to the north, but none to the south. By crossing Throckley Dene where they did, the Romans kept the Wall on the southern edge of this ridge, allowing their men a view to the north from the tops of their turrets and milecastle gateways,[13] while still preserving their main view to the south. The selection of such an extreme solution for their crossing-point, though, may illustrate the importance to the designers of Hadrian's Wall of retaining a view to the south.

From Throckley Dene, the Wall appears to have been planned westwards to Heddon on the Wall and it then turns west-north-west towards the hill on which Rudchester fort later came to be placed. As can be seen from a conserved section of the Wall on the approach to Heddon, Hadrian's Wall makes the turn there in a dip, but my assessment is that the new alignment would have been set out from Great Hill, just before reaching the dip. See Figure 46.

---

13 Visibilities from the tops of turrets and milecastle gateways have been assessed from a height of 25 feet (7.6m). This is on the basis that the upper galleries of the turrets and milecastle gateways would have been at least 20 feet (6.1m) above ground level, and that there would then have been a further 5 (1.5m) feet from there to a Roman soldier's eyeball. In practice these estimates are likely to be slightly conservative.

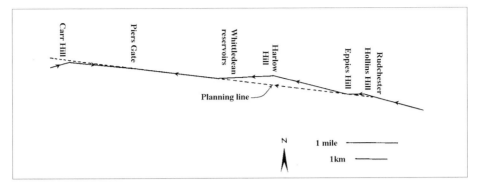

Figure 47: The planning of Hadrian's Wall between Rudchester and Carr Hill.

The new alignment continues past the site of Rudchester fort to a turning point near Hollins Hill. Before reaching this turning point, however, there is a natural sighting position westwards from just west of the later fort's rampart. It appears likely that a long-distance alignment was set out from here, either to Carr Hill, some 6¼ miles (10km) away, or else upon a feature on the skyline near Whittington Fell, 9 miles (14.5km) away. See Figure 47. If this should be correct, then the continuation of the Wall to near Hollins Hill would have been part of a deviation from this line which returned to the alignment quite rapidly at Eppies Hill and then immediately departed from it to ascend Harlow Hill before rejoining the alignment near Whittledean reservoirs. By standing at these turning points it can be seen that the designers of the Wall were deviating to try to gain as good a view north as possible whilst still retaining a view to the south. It would have been quite easy for them, for instance, to have taken the Wall around the northern side of Harlow Hill, and obtained a better view to the north as a result, but they kept to the southern side of it instead.

The Wall rejoins the apparent long-distance alignment just west of the Whittledean reservoirs, and then follows it towards Carr Hill as far as Piers Gate. It will be noticed that there are magnificent views to the south and east from this line, but little view to the north. However, to have followed this alignment past Carr Hill towards Whittington Fell would have taken the Wall across a slight saddle to the north of where Halton Chesters fort later came to be placed. There is no view south from this saddle, and, again, it seems to have been important to the designers of the Wall that it should retain one here. Hence the Roman surveyors appear to have set out a deviation from near Carr Hill to run round by Halton Chesters and then up the watershed over Whittington Fell to Errington Hill. See Figure 48 on page 88. This deviation appears to have been planned from the top of Down Hill; that is, eastwards towards Carr Hill and then Piers Gate, and westwards past Halton Chesters to Errington Hill.

Near Piers Gate the deviation joins the long-distance alignment at such a shallow angle that it is scarcely perceptible, and this is almost certainly the indication of

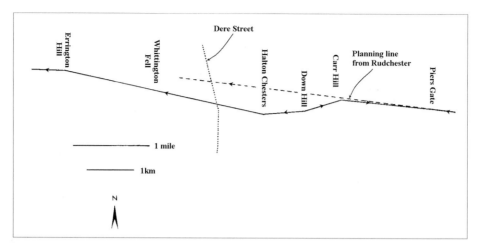

Figure 48: The planning of Hadrian's Wall between Piers Gate and Errington Hill.

an intersection of two alignments planned from opposite directions. The stretch of Wall running from Halton Chesters up to Errington Hill sometimes has better views to the north than the south at ground level, but there would still have been a view south from the tops of the turrets and milecastle gateways spaced along it. These general views can all be checked very readily because the B6318 road (which was the old Military Road of 1761-5, mentioned in Chapter 5) follows the line of Hadrian's Wall all the way from Newcastle to beyond Errington Hill except for short diversions at Heddon on the Wall and around the foot of Down Hill.

At Errington Hill Hadrian's Wall turns almost due west to follow the watershed towards the North Tyne. Then, just above Brunton Bank, it turns at the point where the crossing-point of the river becomes visible and runs straight down to the eastern abutment of the Roman bridge there. The pattern of approximately equally good views to both north and south continues along this stretch. See Figure 49. From my observations on the ground, all of this length of Hadrian's Wall, from Newcastle to the North Tyne, appears to have been set out from east to west except for the deviation around the head of Sugley Dene, and the eastern part of the deviation past Halton Chesters.

As Paul Bidwell has pointed out, the crossing-point of the River North Tyne, opposite where Chesters fort later came to be placed, is the best position at which the Romans could have chosen to bridge the river for miles around. North of this point is a flood plain, whilst to the south of it there are cliffs on the eastern bank of the river.[14] However, I think that the choice of this crossing-point gave the Romans problems with the line of the Wall running westwards from there. If they had wanted, above all else, to retain a view into the South Tyne valley as they worked

---

14 Paul Bidwell pers. comm.

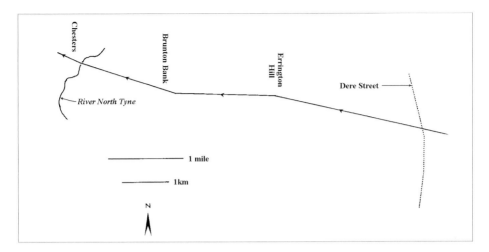

Figure 49: The planning of Hadrian's Wall from Errington Hill to the bridge over the River North Tyne at Chesters.

westwards from Chesters, they would have had to take the line of the Wall far to the south after crossing the North Tyne. Instead, from the crossing-point, the most direct line to take westwards would have been straight up Walwick Fell past Tower Tye to Limestone Corner, and it appears that this is what the Wall's designers chose, even though the view south from this line is mostly very limited. See Figure 50. The view north from this line is generally excellent, however, and this may indicate that in some places the course taken by Hadrian's Wall had to be a compromise between more than one objective. As we shall see in Chapter 11, the Romans may have satisfied their south-facing objective here via a different stratagem.

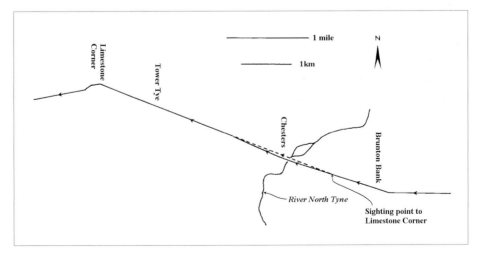

Figure 50: The planning of Hadrian's Wall, restarting from the east side of the North Tyne up to Limestone Corner.

The planning of the line up to Tower Tye and Limestone Corner is most interesting and it took me many visits to the area before I unravelled what I think the Roman surveyors may have been doing. Limestone Corner is clearly visible from where the line of the Wall turns above Brunton Bank, on the eastern side of the River North Tyne. In the normal process of Roman planning, I would have expected the surveyors to have set out an alignment directly from this point to Limestone Corner, and then to have marked out a deviation from it down to the bridging point and then up the western side of the river to rejoin their alignment somewhere near Tower Tye. Instead, it appears that the Roman surveyors on the job had simply walked back up the line that they had already set out from above Brunton Bank down to the river, and then stopped at the point where Limestone Corner first came into view above Tower Tye, and set out their bearing from there. This point lies just above where turret 26B was sited, and about ¾ mile (1.2km) from the turning point below Brunton Bank. Thus the Roman surveyors appear to have saved themselves a walk of about 1300 yards (c.1200 m) uphill, but this also indicates that there had been a break in the planning here. If the planning had been a single exercise, the line to Limestone Corner would most likely have run from the turning point above Brunton Bank. Moreover, the actual line taken to Limestone Corner could not have been set out until the line down to the River from above Brunton Bank had already been set out. Hence, as already indicated, there appear to have been two phases of planning at this juncture: the first phase from Newcastle to the North Tyne, and then the second phase, to Limestone Corner and beyond, which commenced on the eastern side of the River, just above where turret 26B was sited.

At Limestone Corner Hadrian's Wall makes a little detour around a scarp offering a better view to the north without diminishing the view to the south. Limestone Corner is the most northerly point along Hadrian's Wall, and it would be surprising if the Roman surveyors were unaware of this. A new alignment was then set out from Limestone Corner for some 3 miles (4.8 km) past Shield on the Wall, after which a short length carried the Wall up to the location of milecastle 34 near Sewingshields. See Figure 51. The views along this stretch are approximately equal to both north and south, although the South Tyne valley remains obscured from view.

Beyond milecastle 34 the course of the Wall follows an unaligned route along the crags to Walltown. There are generally outstanding views to both north and south along this stretch but it is worth noting that near Steel Rigg, towards milecastle 40, the view from the Wall is notably better to the south than to the north.

West of Walltown the long-distance planning of Hadrian's Wall appears to have been from west to east, and it will probably be easier to describe this framework of alignments first before examining the course on the ground in detail.

From Bowness-on-Solway a long-distance alignment appears to have been set out to the hill on which Drumburgh fort later came to be placed. From this point another long-distance alignment seems to have been set out across Easton

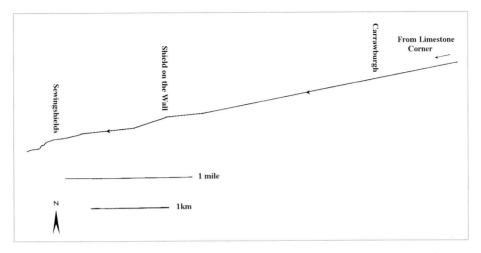

Figure 51: The planning of Hadrian's Wall from Limestone Corner to the start of the crags at Sewingshields.

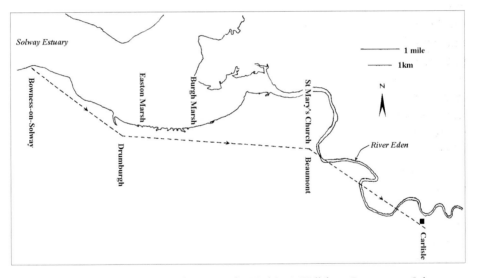

Figure 52: Long-distance planning alignments for Hadrian's Wall from Bowness-on-Solway to Carlisle.

and Burgh Marshes to the prominent knoll on which St Mary's Church now stands at Beaumont. From here it is not conclusive but it seems most likely that a final alignment was set out to Carlisle, not to where the fort is now known to have stood, but a little to the west of it in an area of Carlisle that has been little explored archaeologically. See Figure 52. The direction of planning of these long-distance alignments is difficult to assess, but it seems likeliest to have been from west to east because Drumburgh is prominent when seen from Bowness, whereas there appears to be no significant landmark at Bowness when viewed in the opposite direction.

Hadrian's Wall crossed the River Eden to the north of Carlisle, where there is a significant bluff overlooking the eastern side of the River, and it does seem most likely that the long-distance planning towards Walltown was set out from that point. If so, this would appear to indicate that there were, as to the east of the crags, two phases of planning on this side of Hadrian's Wall: the first from Bowness to Carlisle, and the second from the crossing of the River Eden to Walltown.

In fact, from a study of the topography at the crossing-point, it appears that there would have been a surprisingly good view north-eastwards from the bluff above the River Eden before the area became built up in more modern times. See Figure 53. The first alignment north-eastwards appears to have been set out to Walby, from which point the next alignment appears to have been set out to Chapel Field. From Chapel Field, perhaps surprisingly, the Roman tower at Pike Hill would have been visible, some 5¾ miles (9.3km) away. This tower is one of a small number of such structures that are believed to have been in existence before Hadrian's Wall was built. To have adopted a direct line from Chapel Field to Pike Hill would have taken Hadrian's Wall along the floor of the valley of the River Irthing, however, and it is apparent that the designers of the Wall wanted it to keep to higher ground. Hence it seems that they set out a new alignment from Chapel Field to Newtown, and then aimed for Walton before turning there to sight on the tower at Pike Hill. From Pike Hill it seems likely that they then aimed at another pre-Wall tower at Birdoswald, which would have been visible from Pike Hill. From Birdoswald they then appear to have set out an alignment directly aimed at the foot of the crags at what is now Greenhead Quarry, just west of Walltown. Apart from the planning between

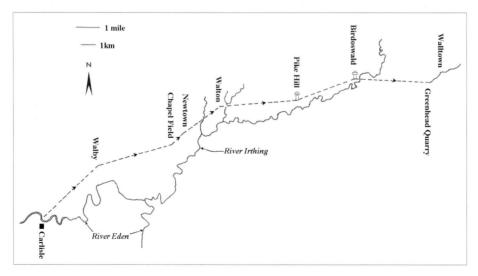

Figure 53: Long-distance planning alignments of Hadrian's Wall from the River Eden north of Carlisle to the start of the crags near Walltown.

the towers at Pike Hill and Birdoswald, which were intervisible, the directions of planning of all of these alignments can be diagnosed as having been from west to east.

We can now return to our tour westwards along the line of the Wall, starting near Walltown at the foot of the crags. From Walltown, the line of Hadrian's Wall as built begins by following the long-distance alignment down to the Tipalt Burn, but then deviates slightly to take advantage of an east-west hollow which afforded the Wall a convenient north-facing vantage position as it runs towards the hamlet of Gap. See Figure 54. Along this length, the land to the south of Hadrian's Wall is, for a change, higher rather than lower than the line of the Wall. However, all of the turrets and milecastles along this stretch of the Wall would have been in sight of the fort at Carvoran, which is believed to have been in commission when the Wall was being planned. From Gap another deviation seems to have been planned, to run up to milecastle 48 beside the Poltross Burn before returning to a local planning line and running onto the shoulder of the River Irthing and turning to cross it by a bridge at Willowford. Apart from the deviation to milecastle 48, most of this length of Hadrian's Wall appears to have been set out from west to east, like the long-distance alignment.

To the west of Willowford, Hadrian's Wall was originally constructed of turf, not stone, and so were its milecastles. Only the turrets continued to be built in stone. As originally set out from Willowford, the line of the Wall ran closely to the edge of the steep escarpment overlooking the River Irthing. See Figure 55 on page 94. However, when the Wall was later rebuilt in stone here, a new course was adopted, a few hundred yards (or metres) to the north. This new course does not possess a view down into the Irthing valley, even from the tops of its turrets and milecastle gateways. Presumably this was not considered important by then, and this point is discussed in Chapter 11.

From Pike Hill tower westwards to Walton, Hadrian's Wall as built (both in turf and then later in stone) does not follow the projected long-distance alignment. Instead

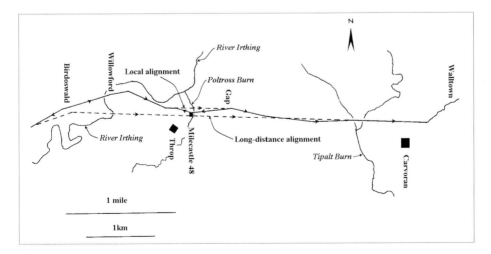

Figure 54: The planning of Hadrian's Wall between Walltown and Birdoswald.

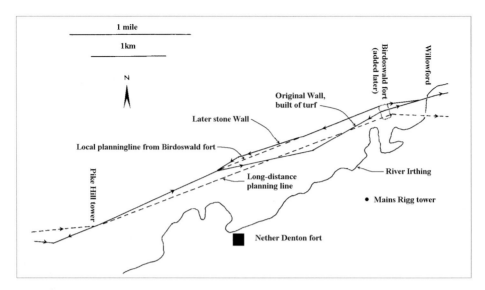

Figure 55: The planning of Hadrian's Wall between Birdoswald and Pike Hill tower.

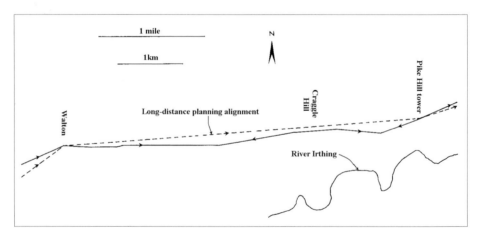

Figure 56: The planning of Hadrian's Wall between Pike Hill tower and Walton.

the Wall follows a series of local planning lines and deviations which seem generally to have been designed to retain a view to the south whilst also securing a view to the north whenever possible. A good example here is the line taken over Craggle Hill, which offers good views to both north and south. See Figure 56. The directions of planning along this stretch vary frequently, possibly indicating the surveyors' efforts to tailor the Wall to the undulating nature of the landscape in this area.

From Walton to Newtown, the Wall's designers had to negotiate the flood basin of the Cam Beck as it flows from the north into the River Irthing. Rather than take to the hills on the western flank of the flood basin, the Roman surveyors seem to have been content to carry the line of the Wall around the low-lying edge of the basin. See Figure 57. This has surprised many students of the Wall because the chosen course

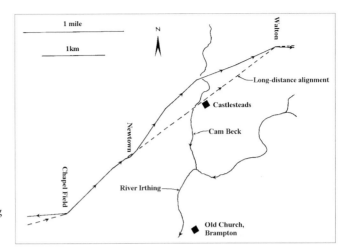

Figure 57: The planning of Hadrian's Wall between Walton and Chapel Field. – N.B. It is uncertain whether the fort at Castlesteads was in commission when Hadrian's Wall was being set out, or whether it was created afterwards.

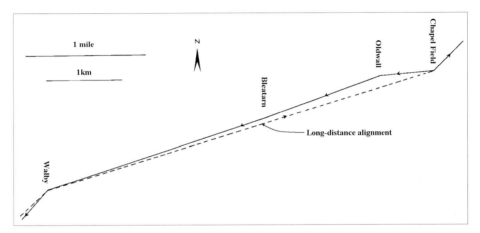

Figure 58: The planning of Hadrian's Wall between Chapel Field and Walby.

here offers almost no view to the north, which could easily have been gained from the adjacent hills. However, as built, the Wall still possesses a generally good view to the south from its lowly position, and, perhaps more importantly, all of the turrets and milecastle gateways along this stretch would have been visible from the fort at Old Church, Brampton, on the other side of the Irthing valley.

At Newtown, Hadrian's Wall regains higher ground and follows a convenient ridge to Chapel Field. This stretch appears to have been set out from west to east, as does the length around the basin of the Cam Beck. Just to the west of Chapel Field, however, the land drops into a short but deep valley, and it seems that the designers of Hadrian's Wall here sought to maintain the Wall's height for as long as possible by following a short spur of higher land down to Oldwall before turning towards Bleatarn and then Walby. This deviation seems to have been set out in the opposite direction to that of the long-distance alignment from Walby to Chapel Field. See Figure 58.

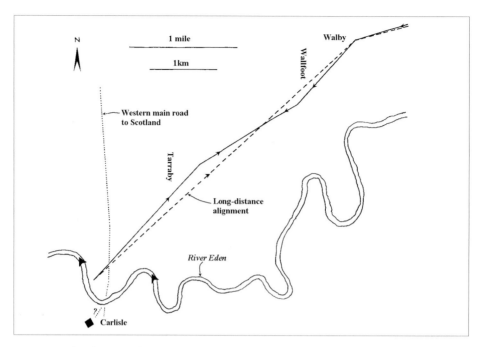

Figure 59: The planning of Hadrian's Wall between Walby and the crossing of the River Eden north of Carlisle.

The land around Bleatarn and Walby is low-lying, with little to obstruct the view either to the north or the south, especially when scanned from the heights of the Wall's turrets and milecastle gateways. Between Walby and the River Eden, however, there are elevated areas at both Wallfoot and Tarraby. The course of Hadrian's Wall deviates from the projected long-distance alignment to take in both of these rises, including running around the southern end of the higher ground at Wallfoot, seemingly so as to preserve a view to the south. See Figure 59.

After the Wall has crossed the River Eden, the pronounced bluff on the eastern side of the Eden shifts downstream to its western bank, and the Wall heads for this and continues along it as far as Grinsdale. This is a naturally strong position for the Wall to take, along the river's edge, but as already indicated I cannot diagnose the direction of planning here because the Wall does not follow alignments on this stretch. The Wall then turns away from the river to run along the edge of a shelf overlooking the river meadows past Kirkandrews upon Eden. It then briefly rejoins the bank of the River Eden before then turning away again and heading up to the knoll upon which St Mary's Church stands at Beaumont. Where I can detect a direction of planning along here, it appears to have been from south to north. See Figure 60.

At Beaumont the Wall turns west but does not follow the alignment from Drumburgh very far before turning off southwards to run around the head of the flat valley of Powburgh Beck, which may have been a marsh or even a coastal inlet in Roman times. Possibly for the same reason, it does the same around the

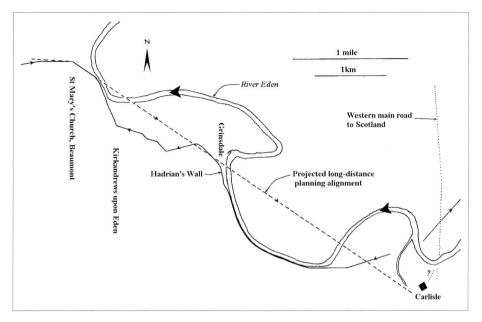

Figure 60: The planning of Hadrian's Wall from the crossing of the River Eden to Beaumont.

head of a small beck to the west of Burgh by Sands, but on the way it appears to execute a rather curious lazy Z-bend through the village of Burgh by Sands, where a fort later came to be sited. See Figure 61. On inspection, it appears likely that the course of the Wall here was set out to run along the southern lip of the higher ground which distinguishes the north of this village from its southern half. It also appears likely that the course of the Wall here was set out from the ends of this Z-bend, i.e. eastwards towards Beaumont, and westwards towards Burgh Marsh.

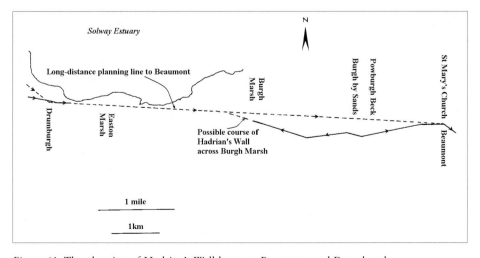

Figure 61: The planning of Hadrian's Wall between Beaumont and Drumburgh.

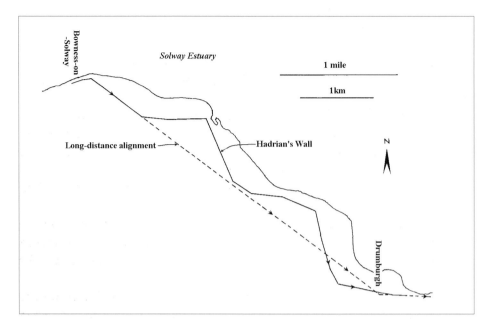

Figure 62: The planning of Hadrian's Wall between Drumburgh and Bowness-on-Solway.

Even though a long-distance alignment appears to have run across Easton and Burgh Marshes it is not clear that Hadrian's Wall did. Recent geophysical work indicates that there may have been some kind of terminus of the Wall at the edge of the modern shoreline at the eastern end of Burgh Marsh.[15] On the other hand, when Francis Haverfield excavated the line of the Wall at the western end of Easton Marsh, what he found appeared to be leading down into the Marsh as far as he could investigate.[16] What is more, the remains that he found appear to me to have been exactly aligned on the projected long-distance planning line from Drumburgh to Beaumont.

West of Drumburgh, Hadrian's Wall pursues a largely zig-zag course along the edge of a coastal shelf towards Bowness-on-Solway, where the Roman fort of *Maia* was later established. The course is laid out in a series of short line-of-sight lengths which have equally good fields of view in both directions at each point of turn, so that I cannot diagnose the direction of planning with any confidence here. However, the final length to Bowness does conclude the course of the Wall by quitting the shelf and following the long-distance alignment for ½ mile (0.8km) into the outskirts of Bowness. See Figure 62. As might be expected, the landscape here is fairly flat, so that there would have been good views in most directions, especially from the tops of the turrets and milecastle gateways spaced out along the line of the Wall.

---

15 Biggins *et al.* 2004, 70.
16 Haverfield 1900, facing page 84; 92-7.

THE PLANNING OF THE VALLUM

Having described at least in outline the planning of Hadrian's Wall, I will now seek to do the same for the Vallum which runs behind it. Again, I shall undertake the tour from east to west.

Between Wallsend and Newcastle, no trace of the Vallum has been found, and as far as I am aware there are no antiquarian reports of its existence. The assumption has to be that the Vallum started at Newcastle, but, as with Hadrian's Wall, my examination of its direction of planning could only begin at Benwell where observations of the best fields of view first become dependable beyond the built-up areas.

From Benwell the Vallum runs straight to Throckley Dene, and it is interesting to note that it does not deviate as the Wall does around Sugley Dene. Seemingly, the cleft of Sugley Dene was of no concern to the planners of the Vallum. See Figure 63.

From Throckley Dene the Vallum runs due west behind Hadrian's Wall to Great Hill, just before Heddon on the Wall, but then makes a rather clumsy double turn before accompanying the Wall on a slightly divergent course towards Rudchester fort. See Figure 64 on page 100. The stretches of the Vallum from Benwell to Throckley Dene and Heddon appear to have been set out from east to west, whereas the stretch to Rudchester seems to have been planned from west to east. Therefore the rather clumsy turn by Great Hill looks to have been a junction between the two directions of planning. We shall see several examples of such junctions along the rest of the course of the Vallum.

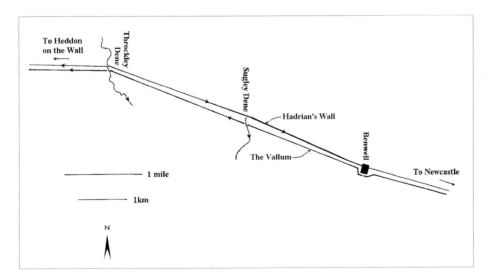

Figure 63: The planning of the Vallum between Benwell and Throckley Dene and on towards Heddon on the Wall.

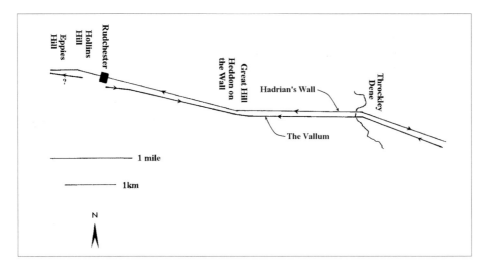

Figure 64: The planning of the Vallum between Throckley Dene and Rudchester.

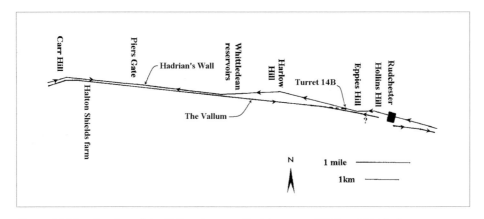

Figure 65: The planning of the Vallum between Rudchester and Halton Shields farm.

West of Rudchester the course of the Vallum is not very clear, but it appears that it may have been planned from east to west. However, not far beyond Eppies Hill, it is met by a 4¾ mile (7.6km) straight length of Vallum seemingly set out from near Halton Shields farm. See Figure 65. The angle at which they meet is very slight, and the point at which they do so is not a natural one from which to have set out a change of direction, being low-lying and with little view in either direction. Hence it appears that this point is likely to be an intersection of two alignments set out from opposite directions. Certainly the line from Halton Shields farm appears to have been set out from west to east, and it is noticeable that it completely ignores the deviation that the Wall makes to Harlow Hill. Indeed, it is possible that this line could have been aligned all the way from Halton Shields farm upon turret 14B, which might have been under construction at the time and which, if so, would have been visible from the farm. See Figure 65 again.

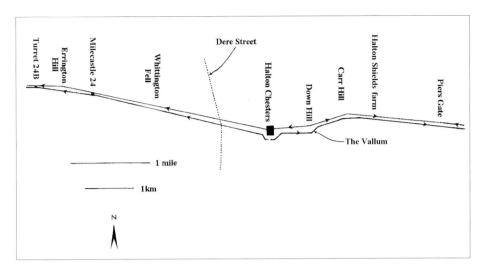

Figure 66: The planning of the Vallum between Halton Shields and Errington Hill.

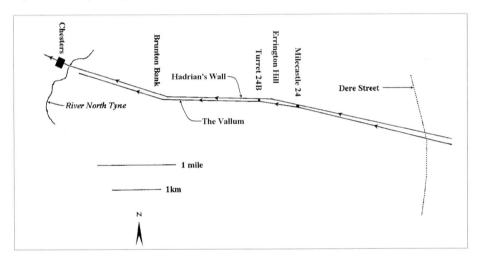

Figure 67: The planning of the Vallum from Errington Hill to the crossing of the River North Tyne opposite Chesters fort.

West of Halton Shields Farm, the Vallum, here surviving in spectacular condition, follows Hadrian's Wall around the foot of Down Hill, and then, after skirting the southern flanks of Halton Chesters fort, ascends Whittington Fell to Errington Hill on a course that converges slightly with Hadrian's Wall. See Figure 66. In fact, by the time it is approaching milecastle 24 near the top of Errington Hill, the Vallum has to take a short cut towards turret 24B seemingly in order to avoid a collision with the Wall. Thereafter the Vallum runs more or less parallel to Hadrian's Wall all the way down to the crossing of the River North Tyne, opposite the fort at Chesters. See Figure 67. From observations of the best fields of view, it appears that the entire course of the Vallum from Halton Chesters to the North Tyne was set out from east to west.

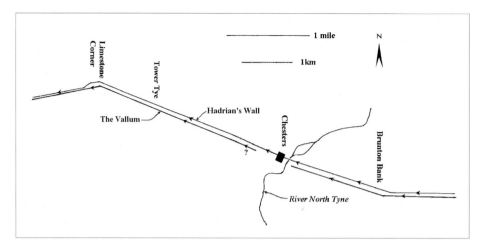

Figure 68: The planning of the Vallum from the River North Tyne to Limestone Corner.

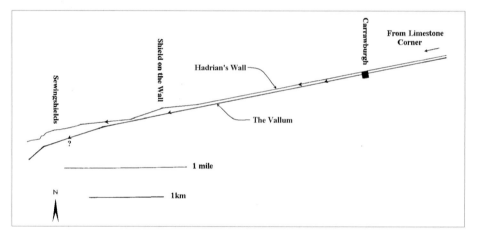

Figure 69: The planning of the Vallum from Limestone Corner to Sewingshields. Note that the fort at Carrawburgh was built on top of the Vallum, retrospectively.

From Chesters to Limestone Corner and on to Shield on the Wall, the Vallum follows the course of Hadrian's Wall fairly closely, except where the Wall makes small deviations to follow the edges of scarps. Although the evidence is largely circumstantial it does appear on balance that the course of the Vallum here was set out from east to west throughout. See Figures 68 and 69.

At Sewingshields, where the Wall takes off to follow its curving course over the crags, the line of the Vallum also turns away, largely to follow a line at the foot of the crags. This line can in places be as much as ½ mile (0.8km) to the south of the Wall, and in the main its course appears to have been intended to elude the myriad bogs and marshes that lie at the feet of the crags. As a result, its planning seems to have consisted of a series of line-of-sight lengths which, from a small number of indicators along the way, appear to have been set out entirely from west to east. Thus, unlike Hadrian's Wall, the direction of planning of the Vallum can be diagnosed between the start and finish of the crags.

What is especially interesting is that a number of the short lengths of the Vallum along this stretch appear to have been sighted on some of the turrets along the line of the Wall. See Figures 70-2. No military advantage can be seen to have come from such an arrangement: it simply appears to have been a sighting convenience for the gangs constructing the Vallum. The turrets may not necessarily have been completed by the time that the Vallum was being set out: scaffolding supporting their construction would have made an equally suitable target, but this does seem to confirm evidence from elsewhere that the Vallum was planned later than the Wall.

To the west of the crags, the Vallum makes a notable detour to the north around Carvoran fort and then, after crossing the Tipalt Burn, makes an even bigger detour

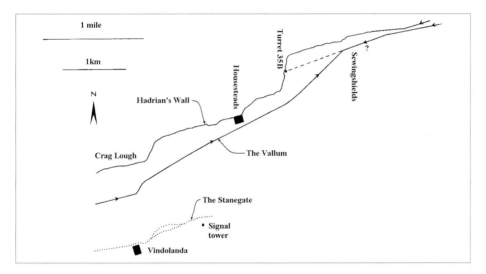

Figure 70: The planning of the Vallum from Sewingshields to south of Crag Lough.

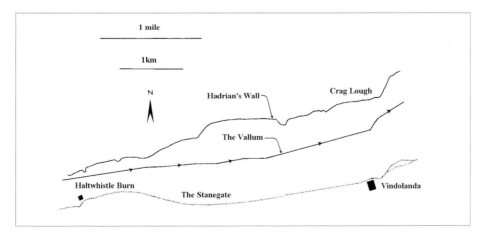

Figure 71: The planning of the Vallum from Crag Lough to Haltwhistle Burn.

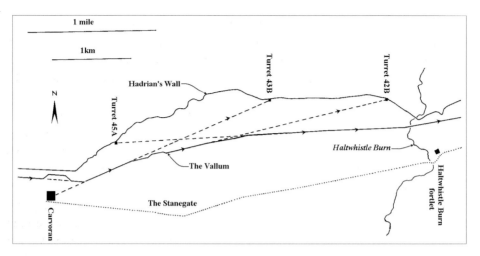

Figure 72: The planning of the Vallum between Haltwhistle Burn and Carvoran, showing some lengths which appear to have been sighted on turrets along the line of Hadrian's Wall.

to the south near Longbyre. See Figure 73. The detour around Carvoran might be explained by the need to avoid a boggy area to the north of the fort, although the area does not appear to be so marshy nowadays. The detour to the south near Longbyre does not appear to be explicable in terms of the topography, and the most likely possibility which occurs to me is that the Romans had planned to build a fort there, nearer the Tipalt Burn than Carvoran. As already indicated, Carvoran appears to have been in commission when Hadrian's Wall was being planned, so it seems odd that the Vallum should then be planned to run between the Wall and the fort unless the fort was intended to be taken out of commission. A fort at Longbyre attached to the Wall would have made a suitable replacement, but it is possible that the Romans then changed their minds and decided to continue with the fort at Carvoran.

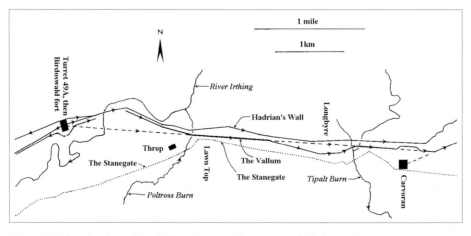

Figure 73: The planning of the Vallum between Carvoran and Birdoswald.

Unlike the pre-Wall tower at Pike Hill, which was incorporated into the line of Hadrian's Wall when the latter was built, the tower at Birdoswald seems to have been abandoned,[17] possibly after the Wall had been planned or constructed. This may offer another connection between the construction of the Wall and the planning of the Vallum, because the line of the Vallum as it descends past Carvoran to the Tipalt Burn appears to have been set out from the turret on Hadrian's Wall that effectively replaced the pre-Wall tower at Birdoswald: turret 49A. See Figure 73 again. This turret was in turn demolished when the fort came to be established at Birdoswald. Hence the line of the Vallum may have been set out in the interval between the abandonment of the pre-Wall tower and the demolition of turret 49A.

The principal reason for using the height of turret 49A (or its scaffolding, if it had been under construction at the time) may have had a closer objective than Carvoran, however. It appears to have been to thread the course of the Vallum between Hadrian's Wall and the line of the Stanegate road, which come close together on the hill of Lamb Top, about 1¼ miles (2km) east of Birdoswald. The convergence of the Wall and the Stanegate on Lamb Top would have been clearly visible from the turret. This alignment, when extended, then carried the Vallum up from the Tipalt Burn past the fort at Carvoran, as noted above. The direction of planning of the Vallum between Birdoswald and Carvoran appears to have been from west to east throughout, even where deviating from this alignment.

West of Birdoswald, the course of the Vallum had to be fitted in between the edge of the scarp overlooking the Irthing valley and the line of the turf Wall, which, as described earlier, was already fairly close to the edge. See Figure 74. However, the line of the Vallum here is squeezed closer to that of the Wall than it

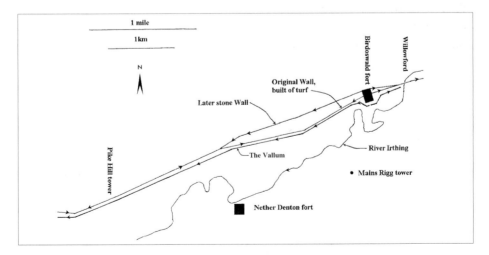

Figure 74: The planning of the Vallum between Birdoswald and Pike Hill.

17 Breeze 2006, 296.

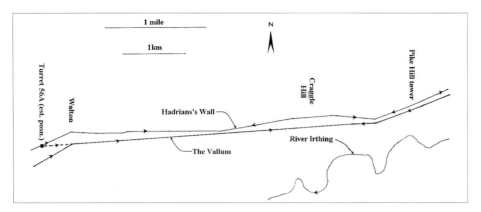

Figure 75: The planning of the Vallum between Pike Hill tower and Walton.

appears it would need to have been, especially around the (turf Wall) milecastle 50. There is in fact ample space for the Vallum to have been sited several feet further away from the Wall if required. The reason for the proximity of the Vallum to the Wall here seems likely to have been, again, in order to preserve a view to the south. To have sited the mounds of the Vallum further away from the Wall would have blocked the view from the milecastle and the Wall down into the Irthing Valley.

Past Pike Hill tower the topography allowed the Vallum to be spaced at a more normal distance from Hadrian's Wall, but between Pike Hill tower and Walton, the undulating nature of the landscape and the deviations of the Wall across it could have given the Vallum's planners, again, a problem in setting out the line of the latter. From Pike Hill to Walton there are several places where the deviations of the Wall would have dipped it out of any long-distance view, and yet it is apparent that the Vallum's planners wished to set out as straight a line as possible for their construction teams, but without colliding with the Wall. To do this it can be imagined that they would have sought to plan from as great a height as possible, and, again, they appear to have used a turret, or the scaffolding surrounding it, for this purpose. That turret appears to have been number 56A. See Figure 75.

The difficulty with this possibility is that the location of turret 56A is only an estimated one. Excavation has failed to find it.[18] However, turret 56A also appears to have been used to set out the long-distance alignment of the Vallum south-westwards to Chapel Hill, and so this does seem to strengthen the case for its deployment. See Figure 76. The upshot of the foregoing planning is that the Vallum appears to have been set out westwards from Birdoswald past Pike Hill to Banks, and that a short junction was made there with the alignment set out eastwards from turret 56A.

The alignment westwards from turret 56A to Chapel Field also appears to have given problems to the Vallum's planners. A direct line would probably have

18 Breeze 2006, 328.

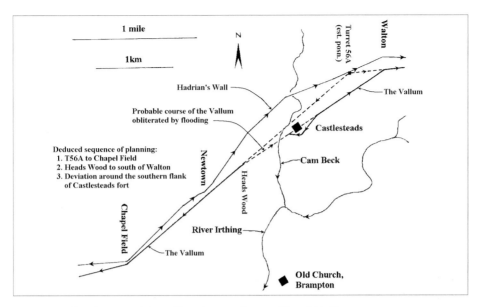

Figure 76: The planning of the Vallum from Walton to Chapel Field.

involved an awkward skewed descent of the east bank of the Cam Beck and it would also have meant passing in front of the fort at Castlesteads. As shown in Figure 76, a complicated set of deviations thus appears to have been adopted here to carry the Vallum around the rear of the fort and then to cross the Cam Beck more directly before re-joining the original alignment at Heads Wood.

The west-facing planning of the Vallum from turret 56A appears to have continued past Chapel Field, but then to have been met near Wallhead, between Chapel Field and Walby, by a planning framework set out eastwards from the crossing point of the River Eden, north of Carlisle. See Figure 77. It is interesting

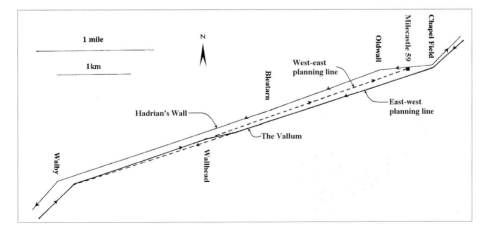

Figure 77: The planning of the Vallum between Chapel Field and Walby.

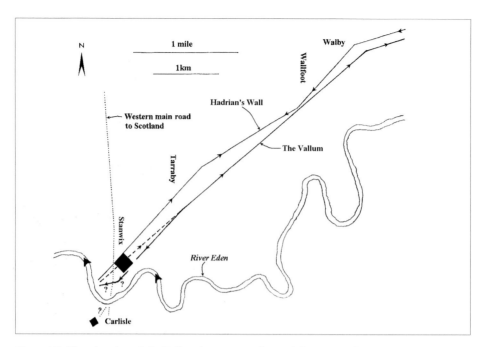

Figure 78: The planning of the Vallum between Walby and the River Eden.

to note that the first part of this framework, seemingly set out from above the River Eden, shaves the line of the Wall very closely at Wallfoot. See Figure 78. A study of the topography indicates that the point of near-collision at Wallfoot would have been visible from a sighting-point above the Eden, and would thus have allowed such precision in planning to be achieved, but only if the walls and the buildings of the fort at Stanwick had not yet been erected much above ground level. If so it appears that the planning of the Vallum here must have taken place before construction of the fort had got much under way.

West of the Eden crossing, the planners of the Vallum appear to have had a similar problem to that already described between Pike Hill and Walton. The line of Hadrian's Wall, often zig-zagging along the bank of the River Eden and then the edges of one or more coastal shelves, would often have disappeared out of sight of any long-distance view across this low-lying but not entirely flat landscape. In order to lay out straight lines for the Vallum, therefore, that would not collide with the line of the Wall, it can be imagined that the surveyors of the Vallum would again need to seek as much height as possible from which to set out their alignments. Immediately west of Carlisle, they seem to have achieved this by using high ground behind where the Cumberland Infirmary is now sited, and then on another high point near Newtown. See Figure 79. Perhaps remarkably, it appears that they also used a long-distance alignment from milecastle 66 at the crossing-point of the Eden to milecastle 80 at the terminus of Hadrian's Wall at Bowness-on-Solway. These two structures, if built or under construction, would have been

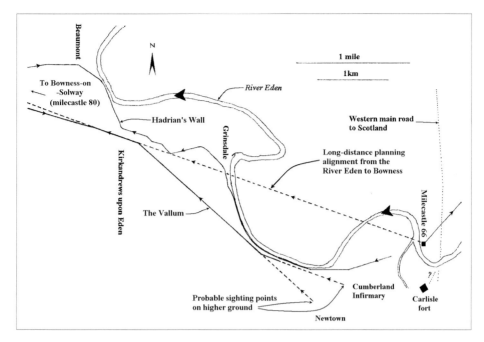

Figure 79: The planning of the Vallum between the River Eden and Kirkandrews upon Eden.

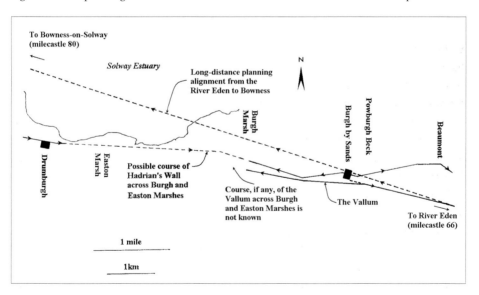

Figure 80: The planning of the Vallum between Beaumont and Burgh Marsh.

intervisible, even though 11½ miles (18.5km) apart, and it would have been a simple matter for the Romans to have verified that the line of the Wall lay north of this line where they wanted to use it for the Vallum. See also Figure 80.

Further west, the Roman surveyors appear to have employed the same tactics, using Drumburgh Hill to set out a line north-westwards for the Vallum that met

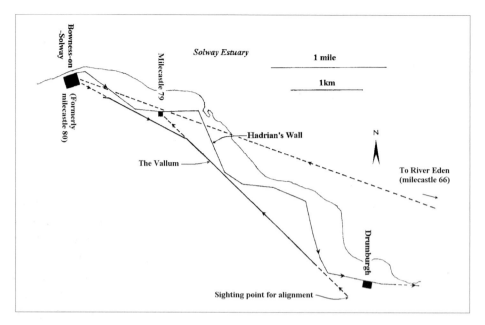

Figure 81: The planning of the Vallum between Drumburgh and Bowness-on-Solway.

a line set out south-eastwards from milecastle 80 just south of Port Carlisle. See Figure 81. As will have been apparent all the way along the line of Hadrian's Wall, except at the feet of the crags, the direction of planning of the Vallum appears to have been outwards from those positions where each of the forts were added (or were to be added) to the line of the Wall.

Before turning to examine these findings to see what they might tell us about the possible purposes of both Hadrian's Wall and the Vallum, it is appropriate to suspend the narrative and make a short digression into the processes by which archaeological data can be interpreted, which is therefore the subject of the next chapter. Those readers who do not wish to disrupt the flow of analysis may wish to proceed directly from here to Chapter 11, but most will probably find it easier to follow the course of the arguments if they accompany me into Chapter 10 first. What is described there is, effectively, an attempt to offer and illustrate a balanced and systemic approach to the analysis of archaeological evidence.

THE ANALYSIS OF ARCHAEOLOGICAL DATA

Amongst the fields of scholarship, archaeology may be unusual in that most of its data is missing. Only a tiny fraction of what would have been part of daily life in the past survives for our scrutiny today. Thus, although glass, pottery, and sometimes metal can transit through time to the present day, nearly all of the organic material from the past such as wood, leather, clothing, food and sometimes human remains are lost to us today unless we are very lucky. Even then, what does remain and become discovered is an accident of survival and may not be at all typical of life at the time.

Hence archaeologists, unlike scientists, have to allocate weight to what has been discovered. Whereas a scientist, at least ideally, might plan and execute a series of experiments to encompass, balance, and compare all the relevant data required to reach a proven conclusion, an archaeologist has to make do with what morsels that time and opportunity have bequeathed to us from the past. It is this ability to allocate weight to the available evidence, and the test of time to prove them right, that marks out the great archaeologists – and their reputations too.

In this context, my work on Roman planning is unusual amongst archaeological work in that a significant proportion of the data – the line taken by a road or a wall – is available. Indeed, if the accuracy of the map-making can be trusted where the line is shown as 'course of' or 'no longer visible' on a map, then quite a large proportion of the data is available. What is missing in my case is exact knowledge of the vegetation in the landscape at the time, such as the extent and whereabouts of woodland and trees, and the dispositions of undrained areas such as marshes and bogs. Yet even with the presence of so much physical data, when it comes to the interpretation of not just what the surveyors of Roman roads and walls were trying to do, but why, then all this evidence is circumstantial. We do not have documents that report what the individual surveyors were trying to do along Dere Street, Hadrian's Wall, and the Antonine Wall in Scotland. Thus we do not know their procedures, their taboos, their political situations or the deals that may have been struck, and it is unlikely that we will ever do so.

Therefore our interpretations could always be wrong. This is not necessarily related to intelligence. We can all make mistakes. Clever people can make mistakes, just like anybody else: it is just that clever people make clever mistakes, and the cleverest people make the cleverest mistakes. Hence we need a means of helping us to be wrong less often, and in archaeology a common way of doing this is via the use of models which combine perceptions of ancient peoples' intentions with awareness of the facts.

All archaeologists, in my experience, create and carry round with them models of what things might have been like in past worlds. These models (which are usually informal) are often germinated when the archaeologists start as students, and they become modified and revised over time as learning, experience and new discoveries are brought to bear on them. Nevertheless, because they go so far back in time they are deeply rooted. Moreover, so many intellectual edifices tend to get built upon them that it can be difficult for their owners to change them or to envisage past worlds in any other way than that embedded in the models that they have nourished over the years. Recent developments in the field of management science may be able to assist here in showing how more than one model can be used to help examine interpretations and understandings from more than one point of view.

The approach advocated is to create, deliberately, multiple models of what the parties at the time (the Romans in our case) might have been trying to do. However, the models need to be more than merely a suite of alternative intentions. Each model needs to embody a fully worked-out way of achieving the objective – a mini-system, in effect – that would have been feasible in the circumstances at the time, as far as we know them. The approach then is to consider and compare each of the workable models in turn with the evidence that we have, but – and this is the key point – to do so with equal enthusiasm for or allegiance to each model, to the extent that we would want each model in turn to be the one that we would wish to favour most. In this way the models can be compared objectively with the available evidence, rather than assessed unevenly, swayed and distorted by prejudices from the past.

My analysis of the date of the Stanegate is an example of this approach.[1] Firstly I listed and examined the evidence to see what weight might be applied to it:

- the course of the Stanegate Roman road is only really well known between the River North Tyne and the fort at Nether Denton; on either side of these points its course is either uncertain or unknown, although it does seem reasonable to assume that it did go all the way from Corbridge to Carlisle;
- the dates of the founding of some of the sites along the Stanegate have been established with some certainty by recent excavations, such as the forts at Corbridge, Vindolanda, and Carlisle;

---

1   Poulter 1998.

- the dates of other sites along the Stanegate were established by excavations conducted up to 100 years ago, using the techniques and knowledge available at the time; as a result they must be regarded as less certain;
- on balance, though, it appears likely that some if not all of the forts along the Stanegate were first established by AD 85 or soon afterwards, but that the fortlets such as those at Haltwhistle Burn and Throp were founded later, at some time in the Trajanic or early Hadrianic periods, i.e. possibly from AD 105 to AD 120; this may have been accompanied by a rebuilding of some of the original forts, which took place around AD 105;
- the course of the Stanegate road does not appear to follow long-distance alignments; rather, it curves to run past all of the forts and fortlets with the exception of the fort at Old Church, Brampton, which one of the less certain stretches of the road appears to pass by at a distance of some 500 yards (or metres) to the north;
- the course of the Stanegate, especially – but unfortunately – in the less certain stretches, seems needlessly curved and undulating and does not take straighter and more level lines between Corbridge and Carlisle, the practicalities of which are demonstrated by the Military Road of 1761-5, and the Newcastle & Carlisle Railway of the 1830s.

I then postulated three alternative models and compared them with the available evidence:

Model 1:   the Stanegate road was laid out first, and the forts and then later the fortlets were built beside it;

Model 2:   the Stanegate road was laid out at the time that the forts were founded, and then the fortlets were added to it later;

Model 3:   the forts were created first and then the fortlets were added at places between them, at which time or later the Stanegate was built to link them all up.

All three models are feasible. Comparing each of them with the evidence, and doing so with equal enthusiasm for each, it can be seen that even allowing for the uncertainty about the course of the Stanegate in places, models 1 and 2 appear to be less likely than model 3. The weightiest argument to me is that the course of the Stanegate would have been nonsensical if the positions of not only the forts but also the fortlets had been unknown at the time that it was set out.

To carry this analysis further, it is possible to construct a fourth model. From the foregoing evidence it is conceivable that neither the fortlets nor the Stanegate road were built until around AD 120. This raises the possibility that the building of the fortlets and the Stanegate road could have constituted just two stages in the execution of an integrated plan to establish a frontier between the Tyne and the Solway, and that adding Hadrian's Wall to the system would simply have been a subsequent part of that same plan. Thus, to hypothesise, the plan might have been:

Stage 1:   add fortlets between the existing forts in the Tyne and Irthing valleys;

Stage 2:   link all the forts and fortlets by constructing the Stanegate road;

Stage 3:   build Hadrian's Wall on the skyline in front of the forts and fortlets;

Stage 4:   build the coastal defences, etc.

This is a different model from that which is normally believed. The normal model is that the designers of Hadrian's Wall picked up on some kind of embryonic arrangement of forts and fortlets that had grown up in the time of Trajan, and then converted it into a fully blown frontier at the time of Hadrian's visit to Britain in AD 122. Again, let us compare the models with the available evidence.

Firstly, there is evidence that some of the original Stanegate forts were rebuilt around AD 105, and this perhaps makes it more likely that the fortlets and the Stanegate road were constructed around AD 105 too. This is believed to have been the time when the Roman army ceased to continue falling back from Scotland and had developed a front line, as it were, between the Tyne and the Solway. Secondly, as already noted in Chapter 5, there are indications that there had been an extended period of occupation at Haltwhistle Burn fortlet before it was decommissioned, seemingly when Hadrian's Wall was built, and this suggests that it was more likely to have been established in Trajanic rather than Hadrianic times. Hence the normal model may look the more probable of the two here, on the basis of current evidence.

Although it may not be apparent from the brief summaries of my findings along Hadrian's Wall that are given in the preceding chapter, the approach of creating and comparing models of how the planning might have been carried out was undertaken by me for each stretch along the Wall. The full archaeological report in the BAR monograph gives details of the key models which were compared at each stage, but in practice many more models were created during the analysis process. Most of these were dismissed very quickly as impractical or at variance with other evidence, leaving only the key models to be compared to adjudge the most likely one in each case.

The advantage of this approach lies in its more balanced and scientific stance: all the evidence is gathered first, and then alternative interpretations are analysed as objectively as possible. Moreover, none of the interpretations is ruled out; some are seen as more likely than others on the basis of the available evidence, and the weightings given to it, but if new evidence should appear which renders one of the other options more likely, then that option can be rehabilitated without bringing the whole analysis down – or any reputations to go with it. The book *Rome's First Frontier* by David Woolliscroft and Birgitta Hoffmann is an excellent example of this separation of the evidence from interpretation.[2] The evidence alone is presented in the first half of the book, and all the interpretation is presented in the second half – with the acknowledgement that other archaeologists might differ in their interpretations of what is presented in the first half.

This is in complete contrast to what I call the adversarial stance – the sort of performance which lawyers put up in court, in which all the evidence that supports their client's case is put forward, and if any evidence to the contrary is mentioned by them at all it is only to dismiss it before the opponent's lawyer can gain an opportunity to raise it. Archaeological reports were often presented in this manner in the past, and to my mind, with its unbalanced treatment of the evidence and its lack of openness to other points of view, this style of argument is inferior to the more scientific approach propounded above. In fact, as I indicated in Chapter 6, I tend to distrust archaeological interpretations which are presented in this way – such as, for example, Alfred Watkins's one-sided arguments for ley lines.

Readers might be inclined to pause at this point and ask why I should be willing to believe that the Romans could lay out straight lines of great length over the landscape whereas the prehistoric people could not. Am I, in other words, being fair? The answer, I think, is that the evidence of the Romans' ability is there to be seen on the ground, and the directions in which they did their laying out can, I believe, be detected too. With the prehistoric people in Britain, I do not assert that they could not do it. I think we must be careful not to underestimate their abilities or their incentives. But the evidence that they did do it, following Tom Williamson's work, is not there. Despite my mistrust of Watkins's approach, which encourages me to disbelieve his arguments, it is the absence of evidence that dismisses them, and that is all we can say, I think, about it.

Even if, unlike Watkins, we must be careful not to propel the models before the evidence, there is a more subtle point about such models which can be hard to grasp at first. We need to realise that models are intellectual devices to help us understand what may have been happening in the past. We must not regard them as fully representative of the reality at the time. As Bill Hanson said, memorably, at a recent archaeological conference: there is unlikely to be a single explanation for anything that happened in the past.

---

2   Woolliscroft and Hoffmann 2006. For the avoidance of misunderstanding, readers should note that the title of this book refers to the initial Roman advance into Scotland, not to Hadrian's Wall.

For those of you who wish to learn more about the theoretical basis of using such models, and see how they can be applied in the kinds of management situation from which the methodology was derived, see *Learning for Action: A Short Definitive Account of Soft Systems Methodology and its use for Practitioners, Teachers and Students*.[3] In the meantime I will offer some hypothetical examples of how easy it can be to produce plausible misinterpretations when we only have a fraction of the evidence before us.

Imagine that a team of aliens has managed to establish a satellite in orbit to spy upon the Earth. One thing that they might be excited to observe is how orderly the behaviour of human beings appears to be when they travel about in their cars and other wheeled vehicles. But they would notice two codes of conduct: in most parts of the Earth, people drive on the right, whereas in other areas people drive on the left. Moreover, most of these other areas tend to be in the countries that are peripheral to the main landmasses, such as Japan, the British Isles, Australia and New Zealand. The alien team might conclude that they were looking at the aftermath of a great conflict that had happened in the past, in which the peoples of the main landmasses had forced their weaker predecessors out onto the margins of the available land. Indeed, from looking at the driving in places such as India they might decide that the conflict is still going on.

Imagine then that the team were able to raise the power of their telescopes. This time they might discover that human beings had developed a system of communication called writing. They might not at first be able to decipher what the writing meant but they would soon observe that there were two main systems of writing, one using a large number of symbols, and the other using a small number of symbols but in different combinations. They might decide that the people using the former system had the superior intelligence because it would require more brainpower to memorise all the different symbols. Moreover they would observe that the people who used the multi-symbol system were concentrated in the eastern part of Asia, in what we call China, Formosa, and Japan. At the same time they would notice that invasions of these countries were being undertaken by the multi-combination system, especially in the cities where examples of both systems could be seen flashing at each other in bright lights across the streets. They might also notice an invasion in the opposite direction in the rest of the World, where the multi-symbol system appeared to have some connection with eating establishments. They might conclude from this that a cultural conflict was in progress, and that part of the cultural thrust might have something to do with food. Perhaps the more intelligent peoples in eastern Asia had developed a superior cuisine and were using its attractions to entice other people in the world to convert to their system of communication.

---

3   Checkland and Poulter 2006.

With their more powerful telescopes the team of aliens might also discover that each car which they could observe had an identification plate with a unique code printed upon it. Studying these codes, they might deduce after a while that the characters on them would not only relate to certain places but that they could also indicate the age of the car. By careful classification they might then discern, to their surprise, that there had been a significant increase in the sizes of cars, especially in the European area, over the last forty or fifty years. Nowadays, they might observe, the Europeans do not appear to be that much different in size from people elsewhere in the World, at least in the northern hemisphere. So, some of the aliens may wonder, might this suggest that there had been some massive conflict or epidemic in the European area earlier in the last century that had left large numbers of the population undernourished and physically shrunken?

Living in the World, we know (or think we know) that:

- the incidence of driving on the left rather than the right is indeed a relic of a sustained period of conquest and colonisation that led to the creation of the British Empire, but it was something that was undertaken from one of the peripheral areas by sea, not by force from the central landmass outwards; moreover, the difference in the code of driving was an accident of history, in that when the British decided to drive on the left – at the time when most of the rest of the World decided to drive on the right – the British Empire was still intact, and so most of the peripheral countries were obliged to follow the British way of doing things;

- the difference in the writing systems is historical, going back 2000 years or more, and there is not currently a conscious attempt to supersede one system by another; the lights flashing at each other across city streets are to do with commercial rather than cultural conflicts and in general at present the aims are to promote and relish the cultural differences between peoples, rather than to try to smother one culture by another; this has not always been so on the Earth, however, including in the fairly recent past;

- the size of Europe's inhabitants has not increased significantly over the last fifty years; there was indeed a major conflict in Europe sixty-five to seventy years ago, but this did not last long enough for peoples' physical sizes to be affected, in terms of their bone structures; the striking growth in the sizes of cars is simply a by-product of commercial competition: every time that a major manufacturer such as Ford produces a new model of their Cortina or Mondeo, it tends to make it larger than its predecessor in order to try to gain an advantage over its rivals.

Thus we can see that there can be some elements of truth in these hypothetical interpretations, but that they can easily be warped in their appreciation of the facts, despite being entirely logical in their deductions. Moreover, it can be imagined that the interpretations would be liable to be shaped by the aliens' own experiences. Thus, for instance, if there had recently been substantial conflicts amongst the alien communities, it can be surmised that this would tend to colour their interpretations. As it happens, much of our World's current activities are indeed dominated by conflict, but to a large extent this is commercial conflict, not military, and commercial conflict might be an unknown dimension to the aliens. For comparison, an unknown dimension to most readers today might be the impact that magic may have had upon the behaviours of our ancestors in the past.

In the light of the foregoing illustrations, it may not surprise the reader to note the frequent uses in my text of phrases such as:

- ' It appears that ...' and
- 'Seemingly, it may have happened that ...'

rather than

- 'It was ...' and
- 'It so happened that ...'

Anyone who declares categorically that something happened in the past, and that they know what the reason was, is to my mind being unwise. Indeed, the reader may have cause to reflect on the observation that the people who have the strongest and clearest views on any subject are usually the ones who know least about it. We need to be aware of the limitations of our thinking.

In this context, my own limitation, as an amateur coming into the field of archaeology, is a lack of an accumulation of evidence of the intangible kind, namely: experience. Firstly, in my studies of the planning of Dere Street and the Roman walls, I have only looked at a very narrow subset of the evidence, that is, the alignments of these structures across the landscapes. Secondly, I have not spent a career examining all other kinds of archaeological evidence and thinking – which could extend from seeing artefacts coming out of the ground to dealing with students' queries and unexpected suggestions. Although I have been greatly assisted in my analyses by many leading and very helpful professional archaeologists, there is no way in which I can ever gain the experience that they have, no matter how many times I seek their opinions and corrections, and no matter how many books and reports I may read.

Therefore, although the interpretations that follow are, I believe, entirely logical and fully derived from the evidence I have studied, they could nevertheless not be right, or not all right. Perhaps I should make the point that even though some of my interpretations may differ from those of more experienced archaeologists, it is not my intention to be controversial. I do believe, from what I have seen, that the interpretations that I will offer in the following and succeeding chapters are correct. Nevertheless, despite this, and my best efforts, they could – like any other archaeological interpretation – still be wrong. Moreover, at any time, new evidence could warrant their revision.

With these *caveats* firmly nailed to the mast, I will now seek to navigate the reader through what I believe the Romans may have been attempting to achieve in the past with regard to the designs and purposes of both Hadrian's Wall and the Vallum.

CASE STUDY 2, PART 2: INTERPRETING THE PLANNING OF HADRIAN'S WALL AND THE VALLUM

Why should the Romans have wanted Hadrian's Wall to retain a view to the south whenever possible, and yet have had little concern about the positioning of the Vallum in the landscape? As already noted, the evidence for these features is untypical of archaeological data in that it is nearly complete, all the way along the Wall from Newcastle to Bowness-on-Solway. Let us begin by constructing some models from different points of view.

MODEL 1

As Paul Bidwell has suggested, the line of Hadrian's Wall may have followed the southern edge of the higher ground in order to run where the rock outcrops best.[1] He observes that at nearly every location where Hadrian's Wall has been excavated between Newcastle and the River North Tyne, the ditch in front of the Wall is cut through sandstone. This would have provided a ready source of material for the Wall and minimised the subsequent maintenance required for the ditch. Even today the ditch is remarkably well preserved for extensive lengths between Eppies Hill and the North Tyne. Paul points out that speed and economy of effort would have been major factors to the Roman command when the time came to construct the Wall.

MODEL 2

A second model is that the Romans may have wanted to maintain surveillance to the south as well as to the north. Conditions to the south of the Wall may have been far less stable than the Romans would have preferred, and during any assault from the north along the Wall they would not like to have been taken by surprise at the same time from the rear.

---

1   Paul Bidwell pers. comm.

MODEL 3

A third model could be that the Roman troops, which were largely stationed along the line of Stanegate forts behind the Wall when it was first set out, could have found it easier to spot and intercept intruders on the slopes running down from the Wall, once such individuals had succeeded in scaling it. All walls can be surmounted if people are sufficiently determined, and I think we can accept that the Romans would have been well aware of this when setting out the line of theirs.

MODEL 4

Another model, related to the same thinking, is that the turrets and milecastles spaced out regularly along Hadrian's Wall would have allowed the garrisons in them to spot people climbing over the Wall and then be able to signal to the main troop concentrations along the Stanegate to intercept them and mop them up. In this model, Hadrian's Wall would not just have been an obstacle to passage: it would have constituted a device for bringing would-be interlopers to the Romans' attentions.

MODEL 5

In this model the turrets and milecastles along the Wall would have been intended for observation to the north and signalling to the south, so as to enable their garrisons to observe hostile forces approaching Roman territory and then alert the main troop concentrations along the Stanegate to be ready to meet them when they arrived.

We can now compare these models with the evidence.

Beginning with model 1, the possibility that Hadrian's Wall may have been built where the stone outcropped most readily might indeed fit the eastern and central sectors of the Wall, but the line of the Wall continues to retain a view to the south when west of Birdoswald, where the Wall was built of turf. It might be argued that the decision to build the western part of the Wall in turf was a temporary measure, and that it was always intended that it should be constructed in stone eventually, just like the rest of the Wall. Hence the line of the Wall could still have been guided by the same motive when its course was being planned.

However, when the Romans did rebuild the Wall in stone at Birdoswald, they chose a different line for some distance to both the east and the west of the fort. This suggests that, at least there, the ready availability of stone might not have been a very important factor in the choice of the line for the Wall. A more significant factor, as has already been pointed out, may appear to be that the line of the turf Wall had a view to the south, whereas the later line, when rebuilt in

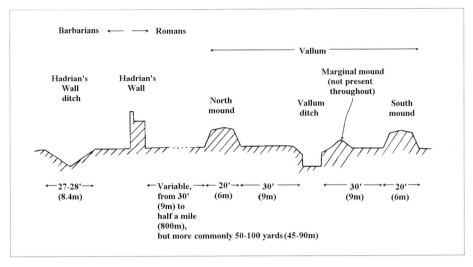

Figure 82: Cross sections of Hadrian's Wall and the Vallum. Note that Hadrian's Wall is shown with a parapet and wall-walk. Not all archaeologists agree with this.

stone, did not. This would seem to suggest that a view to the south was important when the line of the Wall was first set out, and that later it was not. In addition to this point, it is not clear that the most suitable stone did always outcrop along the southern edge of the higher ground, but it might require a geological survey to be sure. It is nonetheless likely that more than one factor might have influenced the choice of line of the Wall, and that this could have been one of them.

With regard to model 2, the possibility that the Romans might have wanted to maintain surveillance of the south as well as the north is a plausible one, and it is strengthened by David Woolliscroft's observations along the Roman road on the Gask Ridge between Stirling and Perth in Scotland. See Figure 1. This stretch of road had fortlets and towers spaced out along it and David found that some of the towers had views to the south-east whereas others had views to the north-west.[2] In other words, it appears that both sides of the road there were being kept under observation by the Romans.

Further support for this idea might come from the evidence that soon after work started on Hadrian's Wall, the Vallum was added behind it, as if to provide cover for the rear of the Wall. The problem with this idea is that the profile of the Vallum is essentially symmetrical, with a central ditch and banks of equal size on either side of it. See Figure 82. As it happens, in places the Vallum's ditch has a slight bank on its southern lip, called the marginal mound. See Plate 23. Therefore, if anything, the Vallum might be seen to be facing slightly more to the north rather than to the south.

---

2   Woolliscroft 2002, 5-6.

Moreover, the Vallum often runs so close to Hadrian's Wall that it might have been, at times, a military handicap. If any hostile forces had succeeded in occupying its northern bank, for instance, they would have had unrivalled opportunities to shoot any Roman soldier on or at the rear of the Wall. In addition, it must be noted that although Hadrian's Wall usually retains a view to the south, it often does not possess a good position for looking down into the valleys of the Tyne or the Irthing and observing movements therein. Rather, it has a good view for looking across the valleys and possibly for signalling to particular points in them.

This might appear to strengthen the case for the fifth model, but let us continue in sequence by examining the third one first. This is the idea that putting Hadrian's Wall on the skyline in front of the Stanegate would allow the Romans below to detect more readily the locations of intruders who had managed to scale the Wall. There are some places along the Wall where this might have worked quite well, but there are others where the Wall is not particularly well positioned to frame the view from the Stanegate. Besides, we do not know the extent of the tree cover in the area at the time, and the idea would not have worked at all in fog or at night, which is when most intrusions might be expected to be made. So this is an idea that might have more of a theoretical appeal than a practical one.

The notion, in the fourth model, that Hadrian's Wall might have been a device for elevating would-be intruders into view from the turrets and milecastles, as they tried to clamber over it, appears to suffer from some of the same deficiencies. If ever the Romans did consider this possibility (and the close spacing of the turrets and milecastles, only ⅓ Roman mile apart, might indicate that they did), then it appears unlikely that it would have been the dominant factor in their planning of its line.

The fifth model proposes that the line of Hadrian's Wall was selected so that the turrets and milecastles along it would be able to observe hostile forces approaching from the north and signal warnings back to the main troop concentrations in the forts and fortlets along the line of the Stanegate. David Woolliscroft has demonstrated that in the central parts of Hadrian's Wall, from Sewingshields to near Newtown, all of the turrets and milecastles would have had (from tower height) either one-to-one visual contact with one or other of the Stanegate forts or fortlets, or that they would have been able to signal to them via a relay tower.[3] I myself checked out some of David Woolliscroft's observations as part of my survey, and verified his findings entirely. The existence of the intervisibilities in each case was quite remarkable.

Further to these findings, it has often been remarked that there are minor differences in the nominally regular spacings between the turrets and the milecastles. Few of the turrets and milecastles, in fact, are exactly ⅓ Roman mile apart. David Woolliscroft has suggested that these displacements from the

---

3   Woolliscroft 2001, 63-7.

theoretically correct positions were engineered so that the turrets and milecastles could in each case be seen from at least one of the forts and fortlets – or their relay towers – along the Stanegate. Since Hadrian's Wall was largely laid out, except over the crags, in straight lines across an undulating landscape, such minor adjustments to compensate for the topography can be expected.

To see if I could identify any pattern in the variations of the spacing of the turrets and milecastles, I analysed the distances between them, and the results are tabulated and discussed in the Appendix. In the end I could not distinguish any consistent patterns in the data, but to some extent this would appear to support David Woolliscroft's suggestion. If the displacements in the positions of the turrets and milecastles had indeed been primarily engineered so as to ensure their visibility from a Stanegate fort, fortlet, or relay tower, then the size and direction of each displacement would have been entirely dependent upon the local topography, and no pattern could or should be expected to be detectable amongst the figures. Hence the results overall seem to lend support to David Woolliscroft's suggestion. However, they do not prove it incontrovertibly since other reasons for the displacements can be envisaged as well, and these may have affected their extent to some degree. These various possibilities are reviewed in the Appendix. Indeed, one reason for publishing this analysis in the Appendix is to let readers examine it to see if they can extract any further information from the spacing than I have succeeding in deducing.

On the other hand, there are some weaknesses with the fifth model. There are certain places where Hadrian's Wall undeniably has a better view to the north than to the south. The clearest example of this is where Hadrian's Wall climbs up to Limestone Corner from the crossing of the River North Tyne at Chesters. The possible reason for the choice of the line of the Wall here has already been discussed in Chapter 9, but the upshot was that Hadrian's Wall was left with little view to the south along this stretch. If the Romans had wanted to signal to the troops along the Stanegate from this stretch it appears that they would have had to rely upon one or more relay stations. David Woolliscroft has speculated that there may have been one such tower on Torney's Fell, overlooking the possible fort or fortlet at Newbrough – although he admits that, on the Fell top, no convincing remains have yet been traced on the ground.[4] Nevertheless, if the Romans should have had such a communications infrastructure in the rear it would have meant that they could then adopt a more forward-facing stance for the Wall along this stretch, and it would appear that they may have taken advantage of this opportunity to do so.

There is a more serious weakness with the fifth model, though, and it applies to the fourth model as well. East of Corbridge and west of Old Church, Brampton, we do not know for certain of any Roman military installations – with the exception

4   Woolliscroft 2001, 72.

of Carlisle – that were in commission at the time that Hadrian's Wall was being set out. South of Newcastle the crop marks of a fort have been observed at Washing Wells, and west of Carlisle a fort appears to have existed by Burgh by Sands,[5] but none of these has so far produced dating evidence that confirms their operational capability at that time. Thus we do not know to what installations the turrets and milecastles east of Corbridge and west of Old Church, Brampton, may have been able to signal. The answer may be that a number of military installations may remain to be found, or that they will have been buried under modern development. Some of these installations may have been no more than signal stations, rather than forts or fortlets, but even so their absence does diminish the case for these two models.[6]

Nevertheless the signalling rationale that underpins the fourth and fifth models does appear to be the likeliest factor to me. Having observed the fields of view at every turn made by Hadrian's Wall between Newcastle and Bowness-on-Solway, it seems to me that the directions chosen by its planners were made on topographical rather than geological grounds, and that the intention was, whenever possible, to retain a view to the south in order to be able to signal to the troops stationed along the Stanegate forts and fortlets to the rear.

So what might this tell us about the purpose of Hadrian's Wall, as originally intended? On the basis of the fifth model alone, the Wall would not have been necessary at all. A chain of turrets and milecastles would have sufficed. In fact, that is what exists down the Cumberland coast from Bowness-on-Solway to just south of Maryport. We have no proof that this chain was erected at the same time as Hadrian's Wall, but the towers and fortlets along it are identical in size, construction, and spacing to those along Hadrian's Wall, and the remains found within them are Hadrianic in date. Hence it appears very likely that they were part of the same plan.

The difference is that they have no wall running between them.[7] Hadrian's Wall starts at Bowness on the Solway and ends at Wallsend on the Tyne. These are believed to have been the lowest downstream points at which the Solway and the Tyne could have been forded in Roman times. Any incursions by raiders into Roman territory beyond these points would have had to have been undertaken by boat. Hence, on this evidence, Hadrian's Wall appears to have been intended to prevent incursions into Roman territory on foot or on horseback.

---

5   Known as Burgh by Sands I fort. For a summary of the dating evidence see Breeze and Woolliscroft 2009, 78.

6   An alternative possibility suggested by David Breeze (pers. comm.) is that the Romans may have intended to build forts east of Corbridge but that this was overtaken by the decision to place forts on the line of the Wall.

7   There has been speculation that a palisade may have run between some of the towers and fortlets along the Cumberland coast, but firm evidence has not been forthcoming. For a review of the possibilities, see Symonds and Mason 2009, 61-2.

Yet a fence, or a ditch like that of the Vallum, could have done this job just as well. Can this, you might ask, have been the sole purpose of something so grand? With its massive construction in stone, its height, continuous ditch in front, and, in places, entanglements of thorns in between, Hadrian's Wall appears to have been intended to be a much more substantial obstacle than this. Granted, it might not have been able to stop an army, but it would have been enough to delay serious assaults whilst the troops along the Stanegate were being mobilised.

It might be helpful, at this stage, to try to model the overall defensive system of which Hadrian's Wall is likely to have been part. Certainly, it did not stand on its own. It can be imagined that there would have been:

- scouting and intelligence-gathering by the Romans amongst the tribes well to the north of the Wall;
- regular patrolling of the land immediately in front of the Wall by the Roman army;
- Hadrian's Wall itself, with its turrets and milecastles, and the Vallum immediately to the rear;
- the chain of forts and fortlets behind, with the Stanegate road running between them;
- the network of Roman roads, harbours, and forts running back across and around the countryside to the legionary fortresses at York and Chester.

This would have been a system of defence in considerable depth, within which Hadrian's Wall would have been only one element. Within such a system, then, can we model what might be the parts that a Wall, such as Hadrian's, might have played?

One possibility – a sixth model, in effect – is that Hadrian's Wall might have been intended to be used as a fighting platform, like a castle wall, with soldiers standing on the battlements fending off attackers below. This is how it is popularly envisaged by many members of the general public. Amongst archaeologists, however, there is considerable argument about whether or not Hadrian's Wall had a wall-walk at all: some believe that it did, whilst others believe that, like the Berlin Wall, it did not.

The course of Hadrian's Wall, as built, might offer some clues here. If Hadrian's Wall had been designed to be fought from a walkway along its top, then the strongest line for it to have taken across the landscape would have been along the north-facing edge of higher ground, not the south-facing edge. The hypothetical line that the Wall might have taken, if it had run along the north-facing edge of higher ground, has been modelled in the full archaeological report.[8] Working from east to west, a comparison between this model and the line of Hadrian's Wall, as built,

---

8 Poulter 2009, 81-3.

seems to show that the north-facing and south-facing lines would have diverged between Newcastle and the River North Tyne, and have done so again from the crossing of the River Irthing, at Willowford, to Carlisle. In between, though, the two lines would have converged and run together: in effect, in the central sectors of Hadrian's Wall, from Chesters to Birdoswald, it appears that the Roman surveyors had managed to find a line for the Wall that accommodated both north-facing and south-facing requirements.[9] Thus it does seem possible that the designers of the Wall might have wanted it to possess some capability as a fighting platform, but that in general they could not give priority to this when other considerations such as signalling to the troops at the rear had to be taken into account.

If Hadrian's Wall had simply been intended to act as a barrier to hit-and-run raiding on horseback – and, indeed, as an obstacle to intrusion, rustling and illicit traffic of all kinds – then it could have been stretched anywhere across the landscape between the Tyne and the Solway. The optimum position for it, though, would have been to run it between the turrets and milecastles along the southern edge of the higher ground. In addition to their rôles for forward observation and signalling to the rear, these structures would then have been best placed to observe would-be intruders trying to climb over the Wall and thus to bring them to the attention of the soldiers to the south. This, you will note, equates to model number 4, above. However, the apparent absence of a continuous barrier down the Cumberland coast and the fact that there are places along the line of the Wall where intruders could scale it unobserved, even from turrets and milecastles spaced only ⅓ Roman mile apart, perhaps indicates that if this was an objective it was a secondary one.

Hence, from the line that it takes on the ground, Hadrian's Wall – when it was first designed, remember – appears to have been intended to fulfil multiple objectives, but it seems that when a compromise in its alignment had to be adopted, because of the lie of the land, then priority had to be given to the need to signal to the rear. Thus we may reach the conclusion that, to the designers of Hadrian's Wall, the functions of model 5 – forward observation and signalling to the rear – appear to have been paramount over the others.

If, nonetheless, the objectives of Hadrian's Wall had indeed been multi-functional, then what might have been the purpose or purposes of the Vallum? In particular, why should it have been considered necessary to add it behind the line of Hadrian's Wall, apparently as an afterthought? Moreover, why should the line of the Vallum, unlike that of Hadrian's Wall, cut across the landscape seemingly regardless of the topography, and why should its course largely have been set out from each of the fort positions once their locations had been decided along the line of the Wall?

---

9   Since the central sectors of Hadrian's Wall are the parts to which most visitors give their attention, this may help to explain why the south-facing aspect of the Wall has received so little notice to date.

1. The western main road (see Figure 1 on page 12) in Bowland. After climbing northwards from Ribchester up to the ridge of Jeffry Hill, near Longridge, this major Roman road to the north then turns north-east across the Hodder valley towards the Forest of Bowland. From the decayed remains of the terrace-way in front of the camera the course of the road continues on a single alignment to the horizon (arrowed), sometimes lost or appearing as no more than a ridge running across a field, but in other places surviving as a hedgerow, farm track, or part of a country road. This is a good example of how a Roman road can disappear completely in some places and then reappear further on, often on exactly the same alignment. Photograph taken in the early 1960s.

2. Double section of the western main road in the Lune Gorge, between Ribchester and Penrith. The further section shows the upper surface of the Roman road, whereas the nearer section reveals the much larger stones and boulders that comprised its foundation. Photograph taken in the early 1960s.

3. Another shot of the foundations of the road in the Lune Gorge, about 1½ miles (2.4km) south-east of the Roman fort at Low Borrow Bridge. Photograph taken in the early 1960s.

4. View north along the Maiden Way (see Figure 1 on page 12) near Meg's Cairn, at national grid reference NY657374. The remains of the road here are believed to be largely as the Romans left them, even though the clearance of some of the rocks along the eastern edge of the road looks to be more recent. Photograph taken in 1975.

5. View south along the Maiden Way from about national grid reference NY658381, approximately ⅜ mile (600m) north of Plate 4. The clearance of the boulders and rocks from the surface of the road remains notable. Photograph taken in 1975.

6. The Military Way below Hadrian's Wall west of Sewingshields. The Military Way is the road built by the Romans to run immediately behind Hadrian's Wall so as to service the various forts, milecastles, and turrets stationed along the line of the Wall. Lying between the Wall and the Vallum, the Military Way is believed to have been constructed when the Romans returned to Hadrian's Wall after withdrawing from the Antonine Wall in Scotland in the AD 160s. To some degree it is thought to have been an emulation of the Military Way with which the Antonine Wall had been equipped from its outset. This is a view eastwards towards Sewingshields, where Hadrian's Wall and the Vallum part company as they travel to the west (see Figure 70 on page 103). Hadrian's Wall keeps to the edge of the crags, to the left of the picture, whilst the Vallum runs nearer the foot of the slope, to the right of the picture, leaving more space for the Military Way to be seen as a strip of green running towards the camera across the hillside. Photograph taken in 1988.

7. Milestone beside the Stanegate at Bradley Burn, close by the Roman fort at Vindolanda. Until the construction of the Military Way (see Plate 6), the Stanegate appears to have acted as the main east-west road in the Hadrian's Wall zone (see Figure 1 on page 12). It seems to have continued in use after the Military Way was built and may well have been maintained until the end of the Roman period. A number of milestones have been found beside it. This is the largest one still standing, as far as I am aware, *in situ*. The course of the Stanegate probably ran closer to the milestone than the modern track curving to the left, but the line of the Roman road may have varied here anyway during the 300 years of its possible operational existence, as forts of different shapes and sizes succeeded one another on the nearby site of Vindolanda. Photograph taken in 1990.

8. The Stanegate about ½ mile (800m) east of the fortlet at Haltwhistle Burn (see Figure 27 on page 49), looking east towards where the Roman road skirts by two standing stones known as the Mare and Foal (seen on the skyline and protected by fencing). The Stanegate here is so substantially-built that it looks almost akin to a railway embankment. Photograph taken in 1990.

9. The Stanegate passing by the fortlet at Haltwhistle Burn (see Figure 72 on page 104). The fortlet was sited on top of the high ground to the left and centre of the photograph whilst the Stanegate (arrowed) can be seen curving around its flanks to run down to a crossing of the burn just off the left of the picture. Photograph taken in 1990.

10. Dere Street approaching the Dry Burn, north of Corbridge (see Figures 19 and 20 on pages 39 and 40). Just before reaching the Dry Burn, the modern A68 road, which has followed the course of the Roman road for some 7 miles (c.11km) from Corbridge, bears off to the right, but this view looking north shows the mound of the Roman road continuing directly on at this point. Photograph taken in 2007.

11. Dere Street at the same point as Plate 10, but looking in the opposite direction and showing the junction with the A68. About 100 yards (or metres) behind the camera, this alignment comes to an end shortly before the crossing of the Dry Burn, having apparently been set out from the village of Esh in County Durham, 26 miles (c.42km) away, in a dead straight line. See Figure 17 on page 36. Photograph taken in 2007.

12. Dere Street climbing up the northern slope of Blackhall Hill in the Cheviot Hills, near national grid reference NT777118. See Figure 25 on page 47. The substantial terracing is well-preserved here, but the blurred edges betray its considerable age. Photograph taken in 2007.

13. Dere Street near Trestle Cairn, about 2 miles (3.2km) south-southeast of Whitton Edge (see Figure 18 on page 37), at national grid reference NT752159. This is the view looking south towards the Cheviot Hills and the border with England. The Roman road does not follow any long-distance alignments through these hills; it simply adopts a curving course suited to the lie of the land. Photograph taken in 2007.

14. The purportedly-Roman road on Blackstone Edge, above Littleborough, north-east of Manchester. Rather than being a relic of Roman times, it seems more likely that the paving is eighteenth-century handiwork and that the prominent groove down the centre is the result of some form of cable operation to winch wagons up and probably down the 1 in 4 (25 per cent) slope on to and from the moors above. Photograph taken in 1965, looking east.

15. The remains of a supposedly Roman road exposed by the Ministry of Works on Wheeldale Moor, some 8 miles (c.13km) north of Pickering on the North York Moors. This view was taken at national grid reference SE804973, looking north-east. It now seems that the apparently excellent preservation of these remains may have had much to do with the unduly creative efforts of the Ministry's curator, and that the 'road' may not even be Roman or a road at all, but a Neolithic boundary bank of the type known locally as a 'cross ridge dyke'. Photograph probably taken in the mid to late 1970s.

16. View of an apparently old road at the former Etruscan sanctuary to Minerva at Portonaccio, near Veii, about 10 miles (16km) north of Rome in Italy. I was given to understand that this was a Roman road, presumably built upon the earlier Etruscan road to the site. This intrigued me because I had understood that even major Roman roads in Italy such as the *Via Appia* had not begun to receive this kind of paving with polygonal stones until the first century AD. Photograph taken in 1989.

17. My curiosity was eased around the corner, where the workmen laying the road had evidently called a halt to their progress for a while. Among other things, this illustrates how convincing the appearance of replicas can be, at times. Photograph taken in 1989.

Long-distance alignment that might have been followed by the Romans

Course taken by General Wade's road

18. General Wade's military road from Fort Augustus to Inverness, looking north-east from a natural sighting-point about 4 miles (6.4km) south-west of Whitebridge. Although Wade's road is clearly following an alignment set out from this point, it only does so as far as the first hill in the middle distance. After deviating around this hill the military road (shown in red) then takes up a new alignment not related to the first, and then curves down to cross the River Fechlin at Whitebridge, after which it takes up another alignment not related to either of the former alignments. This is line-of-sight planning, simply running in straight lines from one intervisible point to another. In contrast, a Roman road in this situation would be likely to have shown greater allegiance to the initial alignment (shown in yellow), possibly returning to it after deviating around the first hill, and then returning to it after crossing the River Fechlin. Photograph taken in the late 1960s.

19. Successive reductions in the width of Hadrian's Wall west of Sewingshields (see Figure 44 on page 80). The foundations of Hadrian's Wall seem to have been intended for a structure 10 Roman feet wide (9½ feet or 2.9m). However, in many places it appears that construction of the original Wall had been interrupted, and that when work resumed it was for a Wall with a reduced width of about 8 Roman feet (around 7½ feet or 2.3m). Later on, an even narrower gauge was used when some parts of the Wall were rebuilt by the Romans, but by then a hard white mortar was used instead of making do with a core of just clay or soil and stones, as had been the practice to begin with. Photograph taken in 1988.

20. Hadrian's Wall approaching its crossing over the River Irthing at Willowford from the east, seen through the trees on Harrow's Scar on the west side of the Irthing (see Figure 54 on page 93). The remains of the eastern abutment of the Roman bridge are nearest the camera, and there is a slight change of direction as the Wall runs onto the bridge, no doubt so as to make the crossing at right angles to the flow at that time. Photograph taken in 1990.

Above:
21. Ditch and mounds of the Vallum west of High House farm, about ⅞ mile (1.4km) west of Birdoswald fort, looking west (see Figure 74 on page 105). Not only the ditch but both the north and south mounds of the Vallum remain substantial earthworks here to this day, nearly 1900 years after they were constructed. Photograph taken in 1990.

Right:
22. At Appletree, 1¼ miles (2km) west of Birdoswald fort, the turf Wall and the Vallum were excavated for the 1999 Pilgrimage of Hadrian's Wall. This photograph shows the Vallum's ditch (partly filled with water) and the north mound, revealing what a substantial obstacle to trespass the Vallum would have represented when first built. See Figure 82 on page 123 for a schematic drawing of the Vallum in section. Photograph taken in 1999.

Left:
23. At Appletree, another view of the excavated Vallum, this time taken from the north mound looking south and showing, respectively, the fall to the ditch, the rise to the marginal mound, and then the rise onto the south mound. The figures on the south mound indicate the scale of the structure. Photograph taken in 1999.

Below:
24. View eastwards along the line of Hadrian's Wall past the consolidated remains of turret 52A, looking towards Pike Hill (arrowed) on which the pre-Wall Pike Hill tower still survives, only 200 yards (183m) away, and clearly out of sequence with the regular spacing of ⅓ Roman mile (539 yards or 493m) between the majority of the turrets and milecastles along Hadrian's Wall. See Figure 55 on page 94. Photograph taken in 1988.

25. Unconsolidated remains of Hadrian's Wall near Garthside, about 1⅝ mile (2.6km) east of Walton (see Figure 56 on page 94). Untouched by restoration, and veined with the roots of trees and shrubs, these remains look a lot less impressive than the carefully manicured parts of Hadrian's Wall that are generally presented to the public, but if you want to see Hadrian's Wall in its natural state today, here it is. Photograph taken in 1990.

26. View looking east from beside the Cleddans Burn, showing the vestiges of the Antonine Wall ascending a shoulder of Hutcheson Hill, between Duntocher and Castlehill, west of Bearsden (see Figure 93 on page 142). The line of the ditch is indicated by the dip in the centre of the slope. The Wall (built of turf or clay and earth) would have stood on the slight rise to the right, and the rise on the left represents the remains of the counterscarp bank. The counterscarp bank appears to have been created deliberately, as an additional obstacle to assault, by dumping the excavated material from the ditch onto its northern side, where the resulting mixture of loose earth and broken clay and rocks would have helped to disrupt charges by would-be assailants before they hit the ditch. Hutcheson Hill has become much more overgrown since this photograph was taken in 1966.

Above:
27. Exposed foundation stones of the Antonine Wall in the New Kilpatrick Cemetery at Bearsden (see Figure 92 on page 141). Although the Antonine Wall was built of turf, or earth and clay, it had a very substantial foundation layer of boulders and cobbles, as this photograph shows. In contrast, the turf Wall part of Hadrian's Wall generally seems not to have had a stone foundation layer, and it is suggested that its durability may have suffered in consequence. Photograph taken in 2001.

Left:
28. Another section of the foundation layer of the Antonine Wall exposed in New Kilpatrick Cemetery, showing the carefully laid kerb stones and a culvert to let water escape from one side of the Wall to the other. Again, the turf Wall part of Hadrian's Wall, at least in the original scheme, appears to have lacked provision for such drainage on a regular basis, and it seems likely that by the time the Romans came to build the Antonine Wall they had become acquainted with the consequences of such an omission. Photograph taken in 2001.

29. The Antonine Wall at the eastern foot of Croy Hill, looking east towards Dullatur (see Figure 90 on page 141). Although much worn down, the massive proportions of the structure can still be gauged by comparison with the domestic buildings on either side of it. Once again, the counterscarp bank on the left-hand (northern) side of the ditch has survived as a larger mound than that of the Wall itself. Since the counterscarp bank comprised stones, rocks, and other material much harder than the turf or clay of the Wall, this is not surprising. Photograph taken in 1966.

Plate 30. The Antonine Wall just west of Rough Castle fort, near Bonnybridge, looking west over the Rowan Tree Burn towards Bonnyside (see Figure 89 on page 140). Not only is the large size of the ditch well displayed here, but the remains of the turf Wall (arrowed) can also be seen standing a few feet high, accompanied by a solitary tree. Photograph taken in 1966.

31. The ditch of the Antonine Wall, looking west towards Watling Lodge, just west of Falkirk (see Figures 88 and 89 on pages 139 and 140). The ditch is preserved to almost full size here and its scale can be judged from the party of Roman archaeologists assembled on its southern edge. Photograph taken in 2001.

32. The Distance Slab found at Bridgeness by the Firth of Forth (see Figure 86). At least eighteen of these carved stone Distance Slabs have been found close by the course of the Antonine Wall, on which they appear to have been erected to mark the boundaries of the lengths constructed by each legion (see Figures 95 and 96 on pages 148 and 149). The Slab found at Bridgeness is the largest of these, being more than 9 feet (2.8m) wide and nearly 3 feet (87cm) high. When found it was cracked across the middle but not smashed, and since it is far too large and heavy to have been readily transported, its discovery is one of the factors that have led most archaeologists to believe that the Antonine Wall terminated at Bridgeness rather than at the fort at Carriden somewhat less than a mile (c.1.4km) to the east. The picture has been kindly provided by David Breeze and is reproduced by courtesy of the National Museum of Scotland, in Edinburgh.

Unfortunately, the directions of the planning of the Vallum do not seem to me to offer insights into what its purpose or purposes might have been. It occurs to me that the directions might, however, give us an indication of how it was intended that Hadrian's Wall should be manned at that time. Conceivably, from the way that the lines of the Vallum appear to fan out from the position of each fort, it seems possible that the auxiliary regiment in each fort along the Wall could have been held responsible for the security of a certain length of the Wall on either side of their fort. However, this is simply speculative, and doubtless other arrangements for garrisoning could be considered.

The line of the Vallum across the landscape, though, does I believe give us an indication of the purpose of that structure. In itself, the line of the Vallum is less well placed than that of Hadrian's Wall to face defensive threats from the north. In addition, the Vallum does not appear to have been designed to possess any signalling function. No towers or turrets are known along it, and the way in which it cuts across the countryside means that it sometimes would have fallen out of view of the forts and fortlets to the rear.

From its line and profile, the Vallum appears to have been intended to act solely as a barrier to traffic. It is noteworthy that it starts and ends exactly where Hadrian's Wall does, with the almost certain exception of the length from Newcastle to Wallsend. Yet its profile is essentially symmetrical, suggesting that it was designed to block traffic in both directions, i.e. from both north to south and from south to north. If Hadrian's Wall had been standing immediately in front of the Vallum, why should the latter have been designed, apparently, to stop traffic from north to south? Two models have been proposed to attempt to explain the purpose of the Vallum.

The first is that when the forts were being added to the line of Hadrian's Wall, the Romans also decided to create a military cordon behind the Wall, bounded by the line of the Vallum, such that this cordon could only be accessed via the forts along the Wall. The other model is that the Vallum was created as a temporary measure because some delay occurred whilst building Hadrian's Wall. Again, let us compare these two models against the available evidence.

A military cordon could have offered some advantages to the Romans. Not only might it have provided an additional line of defence behind the Wall, it could also have provided some protection for the grazing of horses and other livestock, and a safe repository for the temporary stocking of materials, supplies, and equipment useful to the military such as timber, tools, and possibly wheeled vehicles.

On the other hand, the Vallum seems to have gone out of use quite quickly after its construction, in some places. For instance, at Carrawburgh, the fort there, which is believed to have been constructed around AD 130 or shortly afterwards,[10] was built over the top of the Vallum entirely. This may have been only eight years or so after work had first begun on Hadrian's Wall itself, and possibly only six years

---

10 Breeze 2006, 216.

after the Vallum had been completed. Furthermore, when the turf Wall west of Birdoswald fort was rebuilt in stone, the Vallum was not replicated behind it. This rebuilding exercise is also believed to have taken place during the reign of Hadrian.[11] In addition, a military cordon can be expected to have had a fairly constant width, whereas there are considerable differences in the distance between the Vallum and Hadrian's Wall in some places, and all along the way the tendency of the Vallum not to follow the Wall in its excursions to higher ground means that the space between the two of them rarely remains invariable for long. Finally, as far as I am aware, there is nothing like the Vallum on any of the other Roman frontiers, and so if the idea had indeed been to have a cordon, its merits do not appear to have outlasted the first few years of operational experience between the Tyne and the Solway.

The main argument against the second model – the notion that the Vallum may have been a temporary expedient – is its massive construction. Plates 21 to 23 illustrate this. Rather than build the Vallum, it would seem to have been quicker to have completed the Wall anyway. This argument would appear to be particularly relevant in the turf Wall sector, where the Vallum is a significantly larger earthwork than the turf Wall and its ditch combined. See Figure 82 again for a comparison of the sizes of Hadrian's Wall and the Vallum. (N.B. This diagram shows Hadrian's Wall as built of stone. The turf Wall would have been of similar height but wider than the stone Wall at its base – yet still much smaller than the Vallum.)

Archaeologists who have advocated this model of the Vallum as a temporary measure have noted that an interruption appears to have occurred in the construction of the Wall, and have tended to assume that it would have been caused by warfare. In this version of the second model, therefore, the troops would have had to down tools and return to fighting, maybe for two or three seasons. However, a simpler explanation may lie closer to the work in hand. It takes time to build a fort, and all the skilled carpenters and trained stone cutters and masons in the legions who had been working on the Wall may have had to have been diverted to work on the new forts being added to the Wall, and this could have occupied them for a number of seasons in total. This could have left many parts of the Wall uncompleted, and, if so, something would have been needed to obstruct the postulated hit-and-run raiding parties until work on the Wall could be resumed and its full functionality brought into operation. Constructing the Vallum would have been something that unskilled labour could have accomplished, to a large extent, and from the inscriptions found along its length, it appears that the Vallum was indeed built by auxiliary troops. Auxiliary troops were volunteers conscripted into the Roman army from conquered territories, usually overseas.[12]

---

11 Breeze 2006, 60. Hadrian died in AD 138.

12 Nevertheless inscriptions indicate that auxiliaries could sometimes contribute to the building of forts, and therefore they appear at times to have possessed some of the necessary masonry and carpentry skills when required (David Breeze pers. comm.).

A weakness in the foregoing argument is that unless we can accept that little or no part of Hadrian's Wall had been built to full height anywhere before the forts started being added to it, then it would appear that it would have been more economical and quicker to have constructed the Vallum behind only those parts of the Wall that had not yet been completed. Yet the Vallum appears to have been constructed from end to end – or, at least, from Bowness to Newcastle, with only a few places, such as across Easton and Burgh marshes, possibly missing in between. Despite this caveat, I am inclined to believe that the second model is the more likely of the two. The reader is warned, though, that most archaeologists – who possess much greater experience than I – currently believe that the former model offers the more probable explanation for the existence of the Vallum.

Finally, one question which has intrigued both archaeologists and laymen for many years is the extent to which Hadrian himself influenced the design of his Wall. His biographer gives him the credit for creating it, but that could have been no more than a decision to go ahead with it, rather than having a say in the design. Hypothetically, at least, the whole design of Hadrian's Wall with its turrets and milecastles could have been worked out while Trajan was Emperor, and could just have been waiting until Hadrian came to Britain to receive his approval before construction started.

There are, however, a number of features about Hadrian's Wall and the Vallum which suggest that there was someone behind the design who had strong ideas about it that might have appeared better in concept than they proved to work in practice. These include, in the original design for the Wall:

- constructing it so massively in stone;
- spacing milecastles and turrets along it at nominally rigid intervals;
- leaving the main troop concentrations along the Stanegate forts and fortlets to the rear.

It is tempting to allocate these features to the influence of Hadrian. His generals might have appreciated their impracticalities, but by all accounts arguing with Hadrian could be bad for your health, so doubtless if he had been the person responsible for these decisions he would have got his way.

Similarly, if my model of the Vallum as a temporary measure should be correct, the unique profile of the monument together with the fact that it appears to have been constructed all the way across from Newcastle to Bowness-on-Solway, regardless of the state of completion of the Wall, does, to my mind, seem to smack of something designed and commissioned by someone not on site, but not accustomed to being the recipient of dissent. It can be imagined that if Hadrian, *in absentia*, had received news of and then reluctantly accepted the advice of his generals that forts should be added to the line of his Wall, and that this would necessarily delay its completion, he would be inclined to specify exactly what temporary measure should be put in place, the form it should take, and where it should go – and not be ready to brook any further opposition.

This is all supposition. As David Breeze remarked recently, we do not know for certain if Hadrian did influence the design of his Wall, and we probably will never know.[13] The weakness in my own speculation is that all of the ostensibly silly bits are assigned to interference by Hadrian. This not dissimilar to resorting to the intervention of the Fairy Godmother in a pantomime whenever the going gets tricky. Nonetheless the suggestions are left for the reader's consideration.

---

13 For a thorough-going review of the evidence see Breeze, 2009.

CASE STUDY 3, PART 1: THE PLANNING OF THE ANTONINE WALL IN SCOTLAND

In the light of the surprises occasioned by my application of the 'best field of view' test upon the lines of Hadrian's Wall and the Vallum, I was invited by David Breeze to see if my methodology could be applied to the Antonine Wall in Scotland. This Roman Wall runs from Bo'ness on the Firth of Forth in the east to Old Kilpatrick on the north bank of the River Clyde to the west. See Figure 83. Plates 26 to 32 show some features of interest to be seen along the course of the Wall, travelling from west to east. Work on building it seems to have started about 20 years after work had begun upon Hadrian's Wall. Unlike Hadrian's Wall, the Antonine Wall was built of turf and clay throughout, not stone, apart from a foundation layer of kerbstones and large cobbles (see Plates 27 and 28). Like Hadrian's Wall, however, it had a ditch in front – in many places substantially larger than the one on Hadrian's Wall[1] – and rows of entanglements (thorns) placed on the berm between the Wall and its ditch have been recorded in several places.

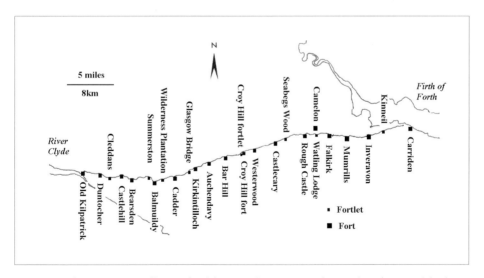

Figure 83: The Antonine Wall in its final form, with primary and secondary forts, and fortlets.

---

1   See, for instance, Plates 30 and 31.

In contrast to Hadrian's Wall, as much as a third of the course of the Antonine Wall lies under urban development and modern roads, and a lesser proportion of its length is visible today. Its course was recorded on the Ordnance Survey Map of the Antonine Wall, at 2½ inches to the mile, and published in 1969, but since that time several discoveries and revisions to interpretation had been made, so that that map was no longer really adequate for my purposes. Fortunately, in connection with what was to prove a successful bid to secure a World Heritage Site status for the Antonine Wall, Historic Scotland had commissioned new maps of the Antonine Wall from the Royal Commission on the Ancient and Historical Monuments of Scotland (RCAHMS). These were the maps, published in 2007 and 2008, at scales of 1:5000 and 1:25,000 respectively, that I used in my survey.[2] The line of the Antonine Wall is much more sinuous than that of Hadrian's Wall, but, fortunately, the new maps showed the line to consist of a series of straight kinks rather than a sequence of curves. As explained in Chapter 3, this meant that my methodology could be used on this Roman Wall, whereas if the course of the Antonine Wall had been a series of curves then my methodology could have produced only indicative results at best.

As before, with Dere Street, and Hadrian's Wall and the Vallum, I identified all of the places on the new maps where the Antonine Wall was shown as changing direction. I then visited all those places that were accessible to the public and which were not built over, or which were apparently closely followed by modern roads, and assessed the fields of view at each point of turn. This exercise was undertaken in September 2008. The lengths thus surveyed amounted to about 47 per cent of the total length of the Wall. Apart from those stretches which were considered to be followed by modern roads, some 24 per cent of the total length of the Wall lay at the time under built-up areas and was therefore not amenable to assessment via the 'best field of view' test. The remaining lengths, which ran over private land, comprised chiefly the stretch between Glasgow Bridge and the New Kilpatrick Cemetery, east of Bearsden. These were kept in reserve so as to be able to test out ideas that might arise from the interpretation of the initial observations. As it happens, there proved to be no need to tap into this reserve. The results from my initial observations were sufficient for me to reach conclusions about the planning of the Antonine Wall – but, again, in a way that proved surprising.

Following my work on the ground, I began my analysis by looking on the maps for signs of any long-distance alignments that might be underpinning the course of the Wall. It was the discovery of the frameworks of such alignments under the line of Hadrian's Wall that had enabled me to diagnose its directions of planning. After repeated examination, and discounting a couple of faint possibilities, I had to conclude that there were not any long-distance alignments that had underpinned the course of the Antonine Wall. Instead, the course of the Antonine Wall appeared to have been a continuous chain of deviations.

2   RCAHMS 2007 and 2008.

To illustrate my reasons for this deduction, we need to return to Hadrian's Wall. Although the directions of planning of the long-distance alignments on Hadrian's Wall could be derived fairly clearly, the directions of planning of the deviations were often more obscure. The main problem was that along a deviation the views would be equally good in either direction at each point of turn. This was only to be expected: when surveyors are setting out short-distance alignments to get around some obstacle or to achieve some local objective, the long-range views are less important. The surveyors will be concentrating upon setting out lines from one point to another which will in the main be intervisible. Two examples drawn from Hadrian's Wall will illustrate this point.

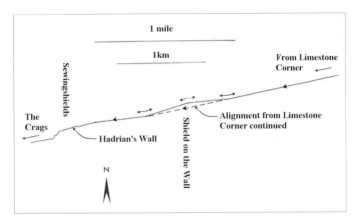

Figure 84: The deviation of Hadrian's Wall at Shield on the Wall, showing equally-good views in both directions at each point of turn.

The first of these occurs west of Limestone Corner, at Shield on the Wall, where Hadrian's Wall takes advantage of a small scarp to protrude a little to the north without sacrificing a view to the south. See Figure 84. The course of the Wall around the scarp appears to be a short deviation from the long-distance alignment running westwards from Limestone Corner. Although the direction of planning of the long-distance alignment is clear, that of the deviation is not. Each of the turning points along the deviation is intervisible with its neighbours, and the fields of view at each turning point are equally good in both directions.

The second example occurs at the far western end of Hadrian's Wall, where, after starting off along the long-distance alignment from Bowness to Drumburgh, the Wall then quits this line and to a large extent follows the edge of a coastal shelf overlooking the Solway estuary. See Figure 85 on page 136. At each of the turning points along this coastal deviation, or series of deviations, the fields of view are again equally good in either direction. The result is that I cannot confidently diagnose the direction of planning of the Wall along this stretch, even though the direction in which the long-distance alignment was set out, from Bowness to Drumburgh, can be deduced more clearly.

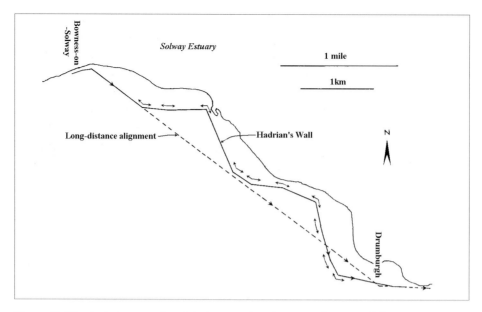

Figure 85: The deviation or series of deviations of Hadrian's Wall so as to follow the edge of the coastal shelf overlooking the Solway Estuary, showing equally-good views in both directions at each point of turn.

On the Antonine Wall, what I found was that the majority of my observations proved to be like those of the deviations along Hadrian's Wall. In other words, in most places where the Antonine Wall changed direction, the fields of view were equally good in both directions. Here and there I was able to obtain some indications of the probable directions of planning, though, but they were not all in the same direction from one end of the Wall to the other. Neither were they uniformly from the centre to the extremities; nor from the extremities to the centre, in the way that Hadrian's Wall appears to have been set out. Instead, the direction of planning of the Antonine Wall appeared to run perhaps 2½ miles (4km) in one direction, and then maybe 1½ miles (2.4km) in the other. This, coupled with the frequency of equally good views at each point of turn, is exactly what would be expected from a series of deviations. As outlined in Chapter 3, one deviation might be planned in one direction whilst another could be set out in the opposite direction. But this then raises the question: if there were no long-distance alignments underpinning the course of the Antonine Wall, then from what would the deviations have, in effect, been deviating?

At this juncture it will be appropriate to undertake a tour of the Antonine Wall, proceeding from east to west, and noting certain features along the way.

The location of the eastern end of the Antonine Wall is not known with certainty. Some archaeologists believe that the Wall extended to the coastal fort at Carriden, a mile or two (1.6-3.2km) east of Bo'ness, although the opinion of the majority is that the Wall terminated at Bridgeness, close by where the Bridgeness Distance

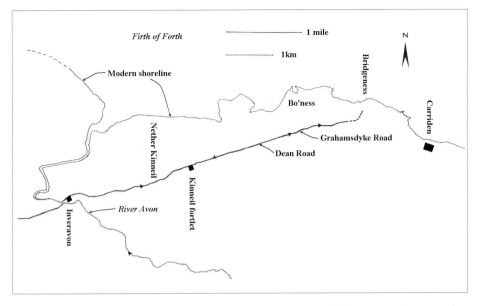

Figure 86: The probable directions of planning of the Antonine Wall between Bridgeness and Inveravon.

Slab was found. See Figure 86 and Plate 32. From this and other Distance Slabs that have been found we know that construction of the Wall was divided into short lengths that were allocated between three legions: the Second, the Sixth, and the Twentieth. It appears that, at the end of each length, the legion that had built that stretch placed one or possibly two ornately carved and inscribed Distance Slabs into the Wall to commemorate their work. A replica of the Distance Slab at Bridgeness has been mounted on to a wall on Harbour Road, close to where the original Slab was found.

If the terminus of the Antonine Wall had indeed been at Bridgeness, then the Wall would have had to climb steeply up to the Grahamsdyke Road, under which its course (or, rather, that of its ditch) is regarded as more certain. See Figure 86 again. Grahamsdyke Road runs west-southwest above Bo'ness along the top of a ridge overlooking the Firth of Forth, making only slight changes of direction as it does so and becoming Dean Road in the process. Westwards from there, unlike the modern road which then turns north, the line of the Wall continues directly on over the flat lands of Kinneil House, passing the site of Kinneil Roman fortlet which has been marked out on the ground with posts, boulders and gravel. The Wall continues past the fortlet right to the edge of the cliff, which may have overlooked the coastline in Roman times, before turning quite sharply and climbing up to the farm of Nether Kinneil. It then generally follows the upper part of another ridge overlooking the Forth, but this time it does so in a series of zig-zags before dropping down to cross the River Avon at Inveravon.

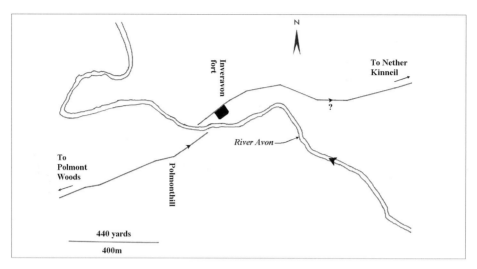

Figure 87: The arrangement of the crossing of the River Avon at Inveravon.

At Inveravon, the crossing of the river is staggered: the course of the Wall to the west resumes about 50 yards (or metres) upstream. See Figure 87. A number of possible reasons have been suggested for this curiosity. To me, the likeliest explanation may be that the Romans had originally planned for the eastern terminus of the Wall to be at the River Avon, but that at the same time they had decided to place some military establishment a little downstream to cover the opposite bank of the Avon, where the fort of Inveravon later came to be sited. So positioned, such an installation would have been in full view of the Roman fort at Mumrills, to the west. If a decision had then been taken to extend the course of the Wall further east, the line would have needed to run in front of the military establishment, so forming the staggered crossing. Moving the military installation might not have been an option if it had been felt necessary to retain intervisibility between it and the fort at Mumrills.

Apart from some indications of the ditch in the Kinneil Estate, the course of the Antonine Wall has remained invisible up to this point, but now the ditch becomes clearly visible as the Wall climbs very steeply up to Polmonthill from the River Avon. The line of the Wall then runs in kinks to Polmont Woods before dropping down equally steeply to cross the Millhall Burn. See Figure 88. From the Millhall Burn the line of the Wall then follows generally straighter lengths before curving south-west to run up to the fort at Mumrills, east of modern Falkirk. Mumrills is one of the primary forts along the Antonine Wall, and it appears that the choice of its position overlooking the Westquarter Burn may have influenced the course of the Wall at this point.[3] In other words, it appears that the position of the fort had been fixed first, and that this had then determined where the Wall should go.

---

3   Hanson and Maxwell 1986, 105-6.

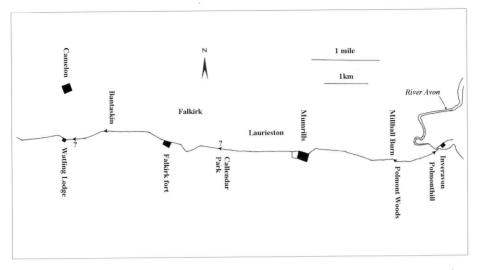

Figure 88: The probable directions of planning of the Antonine Wall between Inveravon and Watling Lodge.

From Mumrills, the Antonine Wall continues fairly directly westwards under modern Laurieston but then emerges into the open, running along a gentle north-facing ridge or slope through the grounds of Callendar Park in Falkirk. Substantial lengths of the ditch are traceable in the Park before the Wall disappears again under modern Falkirk, where the Roman fort was located in an area known as the Pleasance. This fort is believed to have been one of the secondary forts that were added to the line of the Wall after it had been built. The line of the ditch reappears briefly in a housing estate at Bantaskin before emerging much more clearly before the fortlet of Watling Lodge, west of Falkirk. See Figure 88 again. The size of the ditch as the Wall climbs up to Watling Lodge is one of the more spectacular remains of the monument to be seen nowadays (see Plate 31).

Past Watling Lodge the line of the Wall descends sharply to a north-facing edge beside the Tamfourhill Road, and then follows this edge for much of the way to the next fort, at Rough Castle. Through Tentfield Plantation and by Rough Castle, not just the ditch but much of the line of the Wall survives too, as a low mound (see Plate 30). Past Rough Castle, the line of the Wall contours around the north-facing ground past Bonnyside before descending through Milnquarter to the floor of the valley of the Bonny Water, where it takes up station on the same level and course as the Forth and Clyde Canal. See Figure 89 on page 140. Up to this point, the designers of the Antonine Wall seem to have been keen on preserving the advantage of height for their structure, and so this descent to a valley floor seems puzzling, especially since there is higher ground not far to the south. A possible explanation for this is discussed in Chapter 13.

The Antonine Wall briefly foregoes the line of the Forth and Clyde Canal to climb up to the fortlet at Seabegs Wood, but then falls back down to re-join the

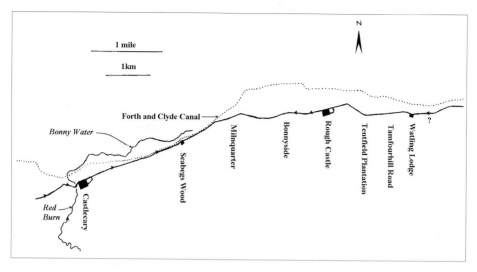

Figure 89: Probable directions of planning of the Antonine Wall between Watling Lodge and Castlecary.

Canal for a short distance before climbing again gently up to the fort at Castlecary. The line of the ditch is visible in places here. See Figure 89 again.

Castlecary is another of the primary forts along the Antonine Wall and, like Mumrills, it seems likely from my observations that its position had been determined before the Wall was built up to it. Immediately west of the fort the Antonine Wall descends sharply to cross the Red Burn, and then climbs equally sharply to adopt a course past Garnhall and the fort at Westerwood. See Figure 90. Along this stretch the Wall generally keeps to the upper edge of a north-facing slope overlooking the valley of the infant River Kelvin.

Past Westerwood the Wall falls towards Dullatur (see Plate 29) and then climbs the eastern flank of Croy Hill, passing the site of the fort of Croy Hill before rising to the Hill's summit where a fortlet was located. See Figure 90 again. Much of the ditch of the Antonine Wall is visible here, and the way that the soldiers had cut its course around the precipices below the Wall seems scarcely credible. West of the crags, the Antonine Wall descends past the village of Croy before climbing again to its highest point, on Bar Hill. Near the summit of Bar Hill, the Wall skirts the remains of a pre-Roman hillfort on Castle Hill, and the size of the ditch just east of the hillfort is again spectacular.

Past Bar Hill, the line of the Wall descends again to the valley floor, at Twechar. This time the valley floor serves as host to the River Kelvin, and again the Wall adopts a line and level not dissimilar to that of the nearby Forth and Clyde Canal past the fort of Auchendavy to near Kirkintilloch. See Figure 91. As before, a possible explanation for this behaviour is discussed in the next chapter.

At Kirkintilloch, the Antonine Wall crosses the Luggie Water, although the location of the crossing-point has not been found. The Wall then climbs up to

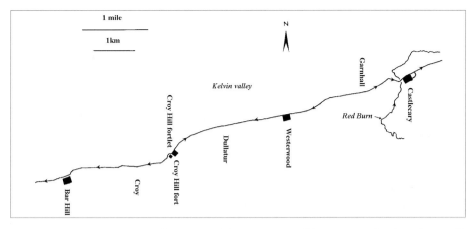

Figure 90: Probable directions of planning of the Antonine Wall between Castlecary and Bar Hill.

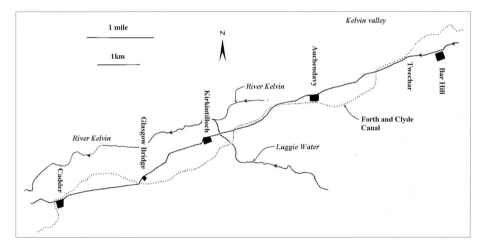

Figure 91: The course of the Antonine Wall between Bar Hill and Cadder.

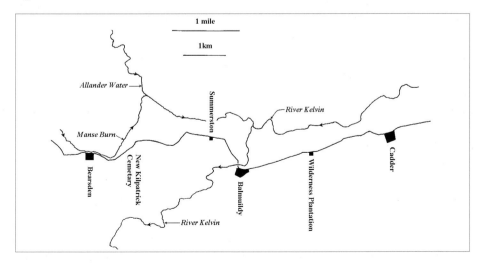

Figure 92: The course of the Antonine Wall from Cadder to Bearsden.

the rock on which the Roman fort of Kirkintilloch later came to be placed before descending again to run past the fortlet at Glasgow Bridge. Thereafter, the line of the Wall pursues an undulating course past the fort at Cadder and the fortlet at Wilderness Plantation to the primary fort at Balmuildy. See Figures 91 and 92 on page 141.

Balmuildy is where the Antonine Wall crossed the River Kelvin, and this time the abutments of the Wall on either side of the River line up with each other – although there is nothing to be seen on the ground nowadays. West of Balmuildy, the Antonine Wall generally adopts a zig-zag course overlooking the ground to the north, running past the fortlet at Summerston to the fort at Bearsden. See Figure 92 again. In the New Kilpatrick Cemetery, just east of Bearsden, parts of the foundation of the Wall have been exposed and can be inspected (see Plates 27 and 28). The fort at Bearsden is another secondary installation and may have been positioned to overlook a bend in the Manse Burn, as it flows first south-eastwards and then north-eastwards through the town in a kind of inverted horseshoe curve.

Continuing westwards, the Antonine Wall climbs out of Bearsden to take in another high point at Castlehill, where a fort later came to be sited, and from which position there are splendid views, especially to the west and south. See figure 93. From Castlehill, the Antonine Wall falls past Hutcheson Hill to the low-lying fortlet at Cleddans before climbing again to cross the summit of Golden Hill Park in Duntocher. Again, there are splendid views from Duntocher, and excavation has shown that the Romans had erected a fortlet there before expanding it into a fort. From this point the Wall continues westwards over higher ground at Carleith before descending gently and finally turning to run into its western terminus, at the fort of Old Kilpatrick. Old Kilpatrick is counted

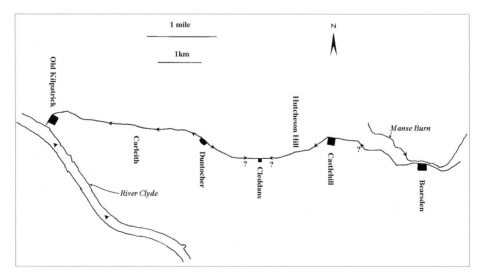

Figure 93: Probable directions of planning of the Antonine Wall between Bearsden and Old Kilpatrick.

as one of the primary forts, and it is even possible that it was in existence before the Antonine Wall was set out. Certainly it was in existence before construction of the Wall reached its perimeter.[4]

From the foregoing, it can be seen that the course of the Antonine Wall is very variable. Sometimes it seems to hold to the high ground as though that were paramount, and yet in other places it plunges down to and runs along valley floors – occasionally sinking even lower than the Forth and Clyde Canal. Moreover, although it rarely runs dead straight for long, there are some places where its course is very direct, whereas in others it zig-zags from point to point as though it were critical to follow a particular contour or edge. Overall, from my observations, the line of the Antonine Wall does not appear to have been the work of a single team of surveyors.

Perhaps the feature that struck me most strongly when I began to examine the line of the Antonine Wall was that its course appeared to curve so as to fall in with the northern ramparts of many of the forts and fortlets along the Wall. This is something that has already been remarked upon at the primary fort of Mumrills (see above), but it seemed to me that this feature applied to many of the secondary forts as well as the primary ones. Indeed, it was something that had first caught my attention when I was marking out all the turning points on the maps, prior to visiting each point to assess the best field of view. When I made my observations on the ground, I noticed that in some places, such as at the fortlets of Watling Lodge and Seabegs Wood, the Wall not only seemed to deviate towards them in plan but that it also climbed up to and then down from them as well. From these and observations elsewhere it therefore appeared possible to me that the locations of most of the main military installations along the Antonine Wall might have been set out in advance, and that the line of the Wall would then have been planned as a set of deviations to take them in along the way.

This notion is contrary to that which most archaeologists believe at present, which is that some forts – the secondary forts – were added to the line of the Wall retrospectively, as the result of a change of plan. This leads to two alternative models.

MODEL 1

The first model – the one which is commonly believed at present – is that the Romans began by setting out the positions of four or five primary forts (including Mumrills, Castlecary, Balmuildy, and Old Kilpatrick), supplementing these with a number of intermediary fortlets, and then running the line of the Antonine Wall between them. In this way the initial design of the Antonine Wall was believed to have been modelled upon that of Hadrian's Wall in its later form, with forts

---

4   Robertson and Keppie 2001, 117.

spaced 7-9 miles apart along its length. Indeed, some scholars believe that, even more like Hadrian's Wall, the Romans may have set out a complete chain of fortlets spaced approximately 1 Roman mile (1.5km) apart all the way along the line of the Antonine Wall. Effectively this would have equipped the Antonine Wall with a chain of forty or so milefortlets similar to the milecastles on Hadrian's Wall. Having first set out the Antonine Wall on this basis, however, it is thought that the Romans then revised their plans by adding some eleven secondary forts to the line of the Wall, possibly replacing some of the fortlets in certain places but occupying new sites elsewhere.

MODEL 2

The second model, proposed from my observations, is that the Romans began by identifying the sites of most of their main military installations-to-be (i.e. both the primary and secondary forts, as well as the fortlets) across the territory to be occupied by the Wall, so that each site would be intervisible with its immediate neighbours. In this way the installations would form a continuous chain able to signal from one end of the Wall to the other. However, in this model, the supposition would be that the Romans commenced construction by building only the primary forts and some of the fortlets in their chosen positions. In the other positions it is postulated that signal towers would have been erected at first, so as to ensure the unbroken chain of communication from the Forth to the Clyde at the outset. Only later, when circumstances either permitted or required it, is it postulated that these towers and some of the fortlets would have been replaced by the secondary forts.

We can now examine how these models compare with the available evidence.

Firstly, experience from Hadrian's Wall and elsewhere does seem to indicate the importance that the Romans placed upon having visible communications between their military sites, especially along a frontier such as the Antonine Wall. In the case of the Antonine Wall, as far as is known, there were no military installations in commission nearby when the Wall was being planned, with the possible exceptions of the forts at Camelon, just north of Falkirk, and Old Kilpatrick, and maybe Carriden. Unlike Hadrian's Wall, therefore, it appears that the military installations were to be positioned along the line of the Wall from the outset. Hence, for the Antonine Wall, the signalling would have been lateral, along the line of the Wall, rather than to its rear. This seemed to be confirmed by my observations that, unlike Hadrian's Wall, there is no sustained view to the south from the Antonine Wall. In fact, with the Antonine Wall there is higher ground, more often than not, quite close to the rear. This observation, incidentally, appears to add weight to my preferred explanation for the south-facing aspect of Hadrian's Wall.

With the first model, any chain of communication along the line of the Wall would need to have been from one fortlet to another or to the nearest primary fort in between. David Woolliscroft has worked out two alternative schemes that forecast where fortlets spaced 1 Roman mile apart could have been sited along the line of the Wall so as to be intervisible with their immediate neighbours, and perhaps courageously, he has provided National Grid reference positions of where such fortlets might be found.[5] The trouble with this model is that so far only nine out of a possible forty or so of such fortlets have been found, despite the predictions of where they should be. Moreover, the nine which have been found do not entirely fit into a regular scheme of spacing 1 Roman mile apart. Somewhere between Kinneil and Castlecary there is a jump of about ⅓ Roman mile (c.500 m) in the spacing, and there is another discontinuity in the spacing to the east of the fortlet of Wilderness Plantation. The existence of the first discontinuity is the reason why David Woolliscroft produced alternative schemes.

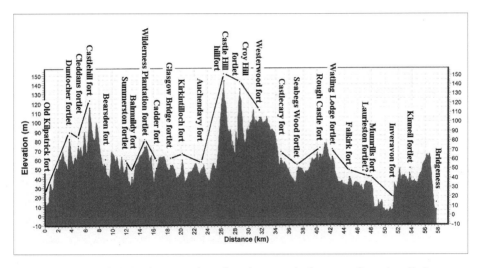

Figure 94: Profile of the landscape in direct lines between the known military installations along the Antonine Wall, showing the intervisibilities between neighbouring sites at tower height, i.e. with eyeballs at 25 feet (7.6m) above ground level. N.B. The profile may not always exclude modern buildings and woodland.

A feature of the second model is that the known military installations along the Antonine Wall – that is, the primary and secondary forts and the known fortlets – are, from tower height, largely intervisible already.[6] See Figure 94. There are a few gaps where discoveries may remain to be made, such as between Castlehill,

---

5   Woolliscroft 1996, 160, 167.

6   It is assumed that there will have been towers over the gateways of the forts and fortlets.

Bearsden and Summerston, and along the easternmost stretch of the Wall from Inveravon, but the recently identified tower at Garnhall would appear to plug the gap between Westerwood and Castlecary.[7] It therefore seems plausible that a signalling chain along the Antonine Wall was created first, before the line of the Wall was set out to link the sites up via a series of deviations. If inter-site signalling was going to be important, it would have been much more practical to have set out all the positions first and then to run the Wall between them, rather than to set out the line of the Wall and then try to add secondary forts to it which (a) covered strategic points, (b) were spaced about 2 to 3 Roman miles apart, (c) were intervisible with their neighbours, and which (d) were also located on the line of the Wall.

This reasoning would still, though, allow two possible explanations for the decision to add the secondary forts to the line of the Wall:

- either: the conversion of some of the initial installations from towers or fortlets to forts could have been intended all along, but delayed until circumstances permitted it – after all, it takes time to build a fort, and it might have been judged more important for the available troops to complete the construction of the Wall first;

- or: the conversion of some of the initial installations to forts may not have been part of the initial plan, but might have been forced upon the Roman command in response to a deteriorating military situation.

To me, there are a number of slight indications that the former explanation may be more likely. Gaps were left in the Wall's ditch, approximately in front of some of these secondary forts, such as at Rough Castle, Croy, and Cadder. It appears possible that these could have been intended to serve as crossing points for the Roman troops when the time came to build these forts. In addition, certain of the alignments of the Military Way which ran behind the Antonine Wall appear to have been set out so that it would become the *via principalis* of certain of these forts, such as at Rough Castle and at Westerwood, when they were built. These indications are, as I say, slight, and none of them is conclusive: the gaps could have been left in the ditch for other reasons, and the Military Way might not have been built before the secondary forts were constructed, or it could have been diverted to run through them when the forts were built. In addition, at the western end of the Wall, it is clear that the fortlet at Duntocher was converted into a fort before the construction of the Antonine Wall reached the site. Hence it is possible that both explanations might have been at work, with events at the time engendering shifts in priorities.

---

7   Woolliscroft 2008.

Nonetheless, whether or not the intention to add secondary forts to the line of the Wall was premeditated or the result of a change of plan, I do believe that it is more likely that the Romans had marked out the locations of the majority of their military installations across the territory at the outset, rather than having to find suitable positions for the secondary forts afterwards. This is especially because of the importance that I believe the Roman would have attached to intervisibilities and signalling. Hence I prefer the second model. However, I do agree that the discovery of more evidence could swing the choice of interpretation either way.

One consequence of the second model would be that by starting at the outset with a complete signalling chain, the Romans could then add the positions of any further fortlets along the Wall on logistical grounds alone. For example, this could have been to plug weak points or to spread the garrison along the line of the Wall. Such fortlets would not need to have been part of an overall signalling chain: they would simply need to have been able to signal to the nearest military installation to raise the alarm locally. If the Romans had chosen to position such additions using a standard unit of measurement similar to that on Hadrian's Wall, then this might explain the locations of some of the fortlets along the Antonine Wall which do not appear to be links in the overall signalling chain. Thus:

- Kinneil fortlet is 2 Roman miles (3km) along the line of the Wall from Inveravon fort;

- Glasgow Bridge Fortlet is 7 Roman miles (10.4km) along the line of the Wall from the fortlet on top of Croy Hill;

- Cleddans fortlet is 1 Roman mile (1.5km) along the line of the Wall from Duntocher fort and fortlet.

However, if the legionaries constructing the fortlets had adopted such a tactic, then they might not have followed any overall scheme of spacing from one end of the Wall to the other. It is possible that they may have opted, instead, to space out their additional fortlets by starting from the locations of the military installations that had already been decided (as part of the overall signalling chain). This could have made more sense logistically. Alternatively, it is possible that, acting independently, the legionaries could have spaced out such additional fortlets from the boundaries of their construction sectors (see below). In either case, this might help to explain the apparent discontinuities in the spacings of the fortlets in places, which has already been noted. However, this is speculation based on very little evidence, and, as with so much about the Antonine Wall, much more data is required if we are to be more confident.

Nevertheless it is interesting to compare my diagnoses of the likely directions of planning of the Antonine Wall with the sectors into which its construction may,

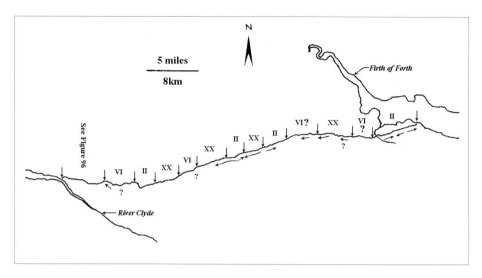

Figure 95: Comparison between the probable directions of planning of the Antonine Wall and the estimated divisions of responsibility for its construction between the Second, Sixth, and Twentieth Legions.

as already noted, have been divided between the Second, Sixth, and Twentieth Legions. The analysis of how the construction of the Antonine Wall may have been apportioned between the legions has been described and published by Bill Hanson and Gordon Maxwell.[8] See Figures 95 and 96.[9] There does appear to be some slight correlation between the directions of planning and the estimated sectors allocated to each legion, although not everywhere. Indeed, an exact correlation should not be expected because the line of the Wall would need to have been surveyed and set out first before the work stints could be divided between the three legions, and we know from the Distance Slabs that the Romans did this very precisely. However, from this it does appear possible that not just the construction of the Antonine Wall but also the responsibility for its setting-out may have been partitioned between the legions. This could help to explain the variations in the directions of planning of each deviation and would conform with the finding from Dere Street that the Romans tended to lay out their deviations at the time of construction, as described in Chapter 4.

---

8   Hanson and Maxwell 1986, 121-30.

9   Figure 96 shows the estimated divisions of construction work for the westernmost section of the Antonine Wall, from Castlehill to Old Kilpatrick. See Hanson and Maxwell 1986, 123. It is possible that construction of this section had originally been allocated solely to the Twentieth Legion but that progress had become delayed by the secondment of part of that legion to fight in North Africa. In order to complete the work as rapidly as possible, it is suggested that construction of this section may then have been divided up between vexillations from all three legions. See Swan 1999, 445. In such a scenario, it seems plausible that the line of the Wall would already have been marked out by the time that the construction work was subdivided between the three legions.

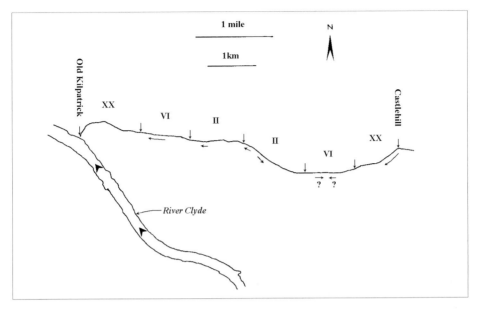

Figure 96: The westernmost section of the Antonine Wall, showing the probable directions of planning and the estimated subdivisions of responsibilities for the construction of the Wall between the three legions – the Second, Sixth, and Twentieth.

Finally, we come to the question of turrets: did the Antonine Wall possess them? As far as I am aware, there are turrets or towers along every other Roman frontier, but none has been found along the Antonine Wall except for the possibility that one may have been built into the fabric of the Wall in Callendar Park. Normally, Roman towers and turrets, if built of wood, would have been constructed on four massive timber posts sunk deeply into the ground. If, however, turrets along the Antonine Wall had been built on post-pads set onto the cobbled foundations of the Wall, and relied for their stability on the turf or clay of the Wall, then they would be very hard to detect archaeologically since so little of the fabric of the Wall remains standing today.

The case for the existence of towers or turrets is not simply that all other Roman frontiers (including Hadrian's Wall) possessed them, so that we should therefore expect them to have been provided along the Antonine Wall. There is a stronger reason than that. The Antonine Wall curves and rises and falls considerably along its length. Even if there had been fortlets studded 1 Roman mile apart all the way along it, there would still have been several stretches of the Antonine Wall where would-be intruders would have been able to climb over it (or under it, possibly, at some of the larger burns) without being seen. The Antonine Wall is such an impressive and expensively constructed barrier that it seems scarcely conceivable that the Romans would have allowed attempts at such intrusions to pass unobserved. Their solution is likely to have been to install either a patrolled walkway along the top of the Wall, or a system of intermediate turrets, or both. Any such turrets would need to have been sited so as to overlook the potential crossing points and to be able to signal alerts to the nearest military installation. From the foregoing, the possibility that such towers may have existed can therefore be judged to be quite high. However, if they should have been buried in the fabric of the Wall and thus only likely to be discovered very occasionally by the merest good chance, how else might they be detected?

I wondered if the line of the Antonine Wall might offer some clues. If, for instance, I should be correct in my belief that the locations of most of the military installations had been determined first, then it is possible that the Romans might also have identified potential crossing points in advance and thus have marked out where turrets should be sited so as to maintain surveillance over them.

I made two attempts to investigate this possibility. In the first I hypothesised that if the Romans had first decided where the turrets should be located, and then set out the line of the Wall to take in these positions, then it could be expected that the line of the Wall would show sharper turns at these points. Hence I identified the sharper turnings along the line of the Wall and analysed the spacings between them. Here and there, some regular patterns of spacing could indeed be observed. West of Rough Castle, for instance, a series of spacings could be identified that were ¼ Roman mile apart, and elsewhere sequences of one fifth of a Roman mile, or multiples thereof, seemed to occur quite commonly. In the end, though, I had to admit that no clear pattern characterised the line of the Wall as a whole.

In my second attempt, I chanced to observe that two stretches of the Antonine Wall in Callendar Park did appear, on the new RCAHMS maps, to be identical in length, at 237 Roman paces.[10] Examining the new maps of the Antonine Wall from end to end, I found nineteen other stretches of the same length, and to me this appeared to be too many to be a coincidence. Might this, I wondered, indicate some module length to which the Romans had been working, so as to place turrets at each turning point? I plotted chains of such module lengths all the way along the line of the Wall and found, to my surprise, that quite often they did coincide with small valleys and other places which could have been opportune places for people trying to cross the Wall unnoticed.

One problem with this hypothesis, however, is the module length of 237 paces: it is not an exact fraction of 1 Roman mile, such as two ninths or one quarter, as might have been expected. Why, therefore, should the Romans have adopted such a length? Secondly, why should I (or the Romans) expect such a module to intercept potential crossing-points along the Wall when their locations would entirely depend upon the topography and not be predictable via any regular system of planning? Further to these points, correspondence with Geoff Bailey of Falkirk Museums indicated that the line of the Antonine Wall across Callendar Park may

---

10 1 Roman pace = 5 Roman feet of 11.64 inches or 296 mm each. There are 1000 paces in 1 Roman mile.

be more complicated than that shown even on the latest RCAHMS Maps, so that having matching lengths of 237 paces could be an illusion anyway. Hence I dropped the attempt as lacking both rationality and dependable evidence.

But even more irrational might have been my aim in looking for patterns in the data anyway. The turrets along Hadrian's Wall were regularly spaced, approximately ⅓ Roman mile (493 m) apart, but for a cross-country barrier such as a wall there is no military advantage in this rigid system of spacing. If my surmise should be correct that on the Antonine Wall the Romans would have located turrets at every potential crossing-point that was not already covered by a fort or fortlet, then I ought not to expect to see any pattern in the data. The distances between the turrets would be determined by the details of the local landscapes, and would be statistically random. This seems to be corroborated by the towers along the German *limes*, which are not regularly spaced.

David Woolliscroft has suggested that there is another approach which could be attempted in order to try to establish the positions of possible turrets along the Antonine Wall.[11] Recent work along Hadrian's Wall has observed that the southern edge of that Wall's ditch might sometimes curve in towards the positions of turrets.[12] It is possible that a close survey of the ditch of the Antonine Wall might reveal similar indentations, and if so offer indirect evidence for the potential locations of turrets. However, I have not endeavoured to undertake this work: it is probable that aerial photography and geophysical survey would be required to support such an investigation.

---

11 David Woolliscroft pers. comm., but see also Woolliscroft 2008, 163.
12 See Hodgson 2009, 26-7.

CASE STUDY 3, PART 2:
INTERPRETING THE DESIGN
OF THE ANTONINE WALL

So, notwithstanding the uncertainties, what can be said about the design of the Antonine Wall?

Firstly, the Roman surveyors who designed the Antonine Wall seem to have appreciated that using road-planning tactics – in the sense of setting out long-distance alignments and then marking out deviations from them – is not the best way of planning a wall. At least, it is not the best way of doing it if the intention is that the wall should be more than just a boundary marker or simply a barrier to traffic. To take full advantage of the ground, in the face of potentially hostile intent, a wall needs to follow the lie of the land more sinuously than does Hadrian's Wall in many places, and the best way to achieve this is to set out its line as a series of short-distance deviations. This is what the designers of the Antonine Wall appear to have done.

Secondly, we have no way of knowing if the Antonine Wall would have been rebuilt in stone if the Romans had stayed longer in Scotland. A stone Wall would have been more permanent, but the Romans do appear to have appreciated that in the short term a better use of their resources would be to build the Wall of turf or clay and put the effort thus saved into cutting a bigger ditch. Hence in both design and construction the Antonine Wall seems to have been created more intelligently than Hadrian's Wall.

To my mind, given that signalling would have been predominantly lateral along the line of the Wall, the main function of the curtain or rampart of the Antonine Wall would have been the same as that on Hadrian's Wall: that is, to stop hit-and-run raiding into Roman territory. Like Hadrian's Wall, the Antonine Wall seems to terminate on the Firth of Forth and the Clyde estuary at points where, in Roman times, it appears that fording on horseback would have become impractical and any raiding beyond these points would have had to have been conducted by boat.

Like Hadrian's Wall, a secondary function of the Antonine Wall is likely to have been to slow down more substantial assaults on Roman territory, in order to allow more time for forces to be mustered in response. Along the Antonine wall, it is noteworthy that nearly all of the forts along it have more defensive ditches on their eastern, western, and southern sides than they do facing to the north. All of the Antonine Wall's fortlets seem to have been protected by ditches around their ramparts, too – unlike most of the milecastles along Hadrian's Wall. These may be signs that on the Antonine Wall the Romans could have faced a more aggressive situation than they did on Hadrian's Wall, and that the designers of the Antonine Wall may have expected that at times its rampart – and possibly its fortlets – would be overrun.

As noted in Chapter 12, one of the striking features of the Antonine Wall is that it sinks to curve along valley floors in certain places along its route, even when there is higher ground quite close to the rear. In some of these places the Wall runs even lower than the Forth and Clyde Canal. It seems to me that a possible explanation for this behaviour could have been that in Roman times the upper valleys of the Bonny Water and the River Kelvin may have been filled in places with marsh and bog. The Kelvin valley is known to have been wet and marshy until comparatively recent times, and in some respects it still is. Facing a marsh, the strongest defensive position for a barrier could, contrary to what might be imagined, have been to site it in the lowest position, right at the edge of the bog, so as to give any would-be assailants no dry land in which to regroup before attempting to storm the Wall. Hence the stretches where the Antonine Wall runs along the valley floors may be those where, in Roman times, the marshes had been at their most extensive.

Finally, we may note that, unlike Hadrian's Wall, but in common with all other Roman frontiers, the Antonine Wall possessed no Vallum. This seems to strengthen the impression that the Vallum was created as a temporary expedient in response to some situation that was peculiar or specific to the construction of Hadrian's Wall.[1] The Antonine Wall seems, however, to have been constructed from the outset with a support road – the Military Way – running closely behind it to service all the installations along its line. This was an idea that seems to have been copied by the Romans when they returned to refurbish Hadrian's Wall around AD 160. Presumably by then the Stanegate road had been found to be too far to the rear of Hadrian's Wall to support effectively those elements of the military operations and installations which had by then been transposed to the Wall itself. This may be another aspect of the superior planning which is apparent along the Antonine Wall.

---

1   David Breeze (pers. comm.) notes that the forts along the Antonine Wall have annexes, whereas there are no annexes (as distinct from *vici*) attached to the forts along Hadrian's Wall. He therefore sees the annexes along the Antonine Wall as taking the place of the Vallum behind Hadrian's Wall.

CONCLUDING SUMMARY

This work stands on the shoulders of others. Not only has it drawn immense benefit from the interest and support of many of today's leading archaeologists – as acknowledged at the outset of this book – but, without the archaeological investigations conducted and documented by their numerous predecessors in the nineteenth and twentieth centuries, it would scarcely have been possible to have reached many of the conclusions reported therein. It would not have been possible, too, to undertake the work without the efforts of the map-makers: those who have scrupulously recorded the courses on the ground of Dere Street, Hadrian's Wall, and the Antonine Wall in Scotland. I do not know the names of those who produced the Ordnance Survey maps showing the lines of Dere Street and Hadrian's Wall and the Vallum, but I am pleased to salute Georgina Brown and her colleagues who, under the leadership of Rebecca Jones, produced the new RCAHMS maps of the Antonine Wall. Again, without the recent availability of maps in digital form, it would have been much more difficult for me to examine the possible intervisibilities of sites across various landscapes. These intervisibilities, the reader will have noticed, have become a very important factor in my arguments and conclusions. Lastly, the motor car – not commonly regarded as an archaeological tool – has made it much easier and less time-consuming, and vastly more practical, to cover the extensive ground repeatedly, if necessary, to make and then verify the body of observations upon which this work is based. It is hoped that this work documented here might, in turn, provide another step upon which future researchers, armed with new insights and technologies, can themselves stand in order to see ever more clearly what may have happened in the past.

SUMMARY OF MY WORK AND CONCLUSIONS

I think my work has introduced a novel means of determining the directions in which Roman surveyors may have been working when setting out the lines of their roads on the ground. The methodology depends upon the presumed behaviour of Roman surveyors when marking out the straight alignments for which they are famous, and experience appears to show that the methodology does work, especially for the longer-distance alignments. The methodology, however, cannot produce dependable results where the Roman surveyors appear to have foregone the use of alignments, or where the course of the road lies under built-up areas where the best field of view cannot be reliably assessed.

Application of this methodology to part of the course of what we now call Dere Street, from the Vale of York to Newstead in Scotland, has indicated that the Romans may not necessarily have regarded this as a single road, and that it was probably set out by at least three separate teams of surveyors working in different directions. Moreover, examination of the courses of deviations from the initial planning lines, coupled with information from archaeological investigations from sites along the way, makes it appear likely that there may have been a period of more than thirty years between the original planning of this road and the completion of its construction.

The practices employed by Roman surveyors when planning their roads on the ground have been examined and shown to be based, typically, upon first marking out a framework of long-distance alignments and then setting out deviations from them to meet local objectives, such as to attain suitable river crossings or to avoid unacceptable obstacles. It appears likely that the deviations were in general only set out when the time came to construct the road, and it also appears that this could sometimes be many years after the long-distance alignments had been marked out. A comparison has also been drawn between Roman roads and their principal equivalents in Britain – the eighteenth-century military roads in Scotland – and it is evident that not just their construction but their planning processes were inherently different. Subjects have also been suggested for future research on Roman roads, including why Roman surveyors should have set out and followed such enormously long alignments. Might these alignments, it is asked, have been more than merely devices for laying out roads? In addition, a question is posed about the disappearance of Roman roads. Why is it that the straighter stretches seem to be the ones that remain in use, whereas the less straight stretches seem to be the ones that become lost over time? What might be the factors at work here?

Application of the diagnostic methodology to Hadrian's Wall has indicated that the planning of the Wall and the Vallum that runs behind it were quite different in both nature and direction. Hadrian's Wall appears to have been planned inwards from the coasts towards the central crags, and designed to preserve a view to the south, whereas the Vallum seems largely to have been planned outwards from each of the forts that were added to the Wall after construction had started, and it tends to cut across the landscape regardless of the topography.

A systems-based methodology for the interpretation of archaeological data has been described, and its application to the planning of Hadrian's Wall and the Vallum suggests that the Wall was designed to fulfil multiple purposes. However, if a compromise had to be reached about where the Wall should be sited in the countryside, then precedence appears to have been given to the need for forward observation, and signalling to the rear, from the turrets and milecastles that were studded along the line of the Wall. As David Woolliscroft has shown, the signalling seems likely to have been back to the troops stationed in the forts and fortlets that were positioned on the line of the Stanegate Roman road that ran along the Tyne and Irthing valleys behind the line of the Wall. In contrast, the Vallum appears to have been intended to fulfil a single function: that is, to block traffic from both north and south. On this basis, the construction of the Vallum has been interpreted as a temporary measure that was adopted whilst the forts were being constructed along the line of the Wall, so forcing completion of the latter had to be delayed.

Application of the diagnostic methodology to the Antonine Wall also produced new findings, but in an unexpected way. Unlike Hadrian's Wall and the Vallum, it appears that on the Antonine Wall the Roman planners did not begin by setting out long-distance alignments. Instead, it appears likely that they first set out a line of military installations between the Firth of Forth and the River Clyde, such that each installation would be intervisible with its neighbours. In this way it appears that they established a continuous chain of communication from coast to coast before setting out the line of the Antonine Wall to run between them. This is considered a more intelligent approach to designing the course of a wall than that adopted on Hadrian's Wall. There the line of the Wall seems to have been set out first and then the final details of the signalling and communications only sorted out afterwards.

In some respects, these conclusions differ from those which most archaeologists presently hold, and so it is hoped that this work will now be received as a contribution to on-going archaeological debate. It is recognised that these conclusions could be altered at any time by further evidence – but this is always the case in archaeological studies. Indeed, it is the fact that I have examined evidence that has been little investigated in the past, and that I have done so in a new way, that has generated these new observations, ideas and interpretations which are now submitted for consideration within the archaeological community as a whole.

APPENDIX

ANALYSIS OF THE SPACING OF TURRETS AND MILECASTLES ALONG HADRIAN'S WALL, BASED UPON THE FIGURES REPORTED BY R. G. COLLINGWOOD[1]

R. G. Collingwood devised a system of numbering for the milecastles and turrets along Hadrian's Wall, working westwards from the eastern terminus of the Wall at Wallsend, and this system has remained in use to this day. Milecastles were allocated whole numbers, and the two turrets to the west of them were given the same number but suffixed A and B. Thus after milecastle 8 there would be turret 8A, then turret 8B, and then milecastle 9, and then turret 9A, and so on. These are the numbers used in column 1 in the table beginning on page 160.

Collingwood reported distances between some of the turrets and milecastles, but not all of them. In addition, some of the positions of the turrets and milecastles that Collingwood reported were only estimated locations, and I have excluded these from the analysis below. These reasons are why there are gaps in the table – for instance, nothing before turret 7B, and then gaps between turret 10A and milecastle 22, milecastle 27 and 29, etc., and then nothing after turret 51B. Hence the table analyses only the reported measurements between turrets and milecastles of known positions.

Collingwood's distances were recorded in Imperial units (yards). From Collingwood's data, the sum of the reported distances between the locations of the known milecastles (8-10, 22-7, 29-31, 36-42, 44-6, and 47-51) is 34,262 yards. The average distance between these milecastles is therefore 1631.5 yards. Hence the average distance between each turret and milecastle if they had been exactly equally spaced should be ⅓ of this = 543.8 yards (497.3 m). This figure has been rounded to 544 yards (497 m), and is used as the mean theoretical distance between each turret and milecastle for the calculations in the table. Using the actual figures in this way avoids making the assumption that the spacing that was used by the Romans was indeed exactly ⅓ Roman mile (539.3 yards or 493 m), although in practice the closeness of the mean to ⅓ Roman mile would appear to support this supposition strongly.

Column 2 shows the actual distance between the turrets and milecastles, as reported by Collingwood. Column 3 shows the difference between the actual distance and the aforegoing calculated mean, i.e. the variance of the actual

---

1   Collingwood 1929-30.

location from the theoretically correct position if all the turrets and milecastles had been equally spaced apart.

Column 4 shows the running total of these variances. Thus, for example, the distance between turret 7B and milecastle 8 is 166 yards greater than the mean, whereas the distance between milecastle 8 and turret 8A is 22 yards less than the mean, so that turret 8A can be considered only 144 yards out of a theoretically correct position, starting from turret 7B. Similarly, the distance between turret 8B and turret 8A is 12 yards less than the mean, meaning that turret 8B can be considered only 132 yards out of position, starting from turret 7B. Since we do not have information about where the Roman datum (starting position) may have been, i.e. the point from which they may have measured their distances, we have little option but to take the location of any turret or milecastle in each group as the starting position in order to be able to analyse this cumulative displacement from the norm, and to see what we can make of the information to be gained from it. For this purpose, taking the location of the first turret or milecastle in each group is as good as taking any other.

Columns 5, 6, and 7 are simply conversions, from Imperial units to metric, of columns 2, 3, and 4, rounded to the nearest metre.

Milecastle and Turret No.	Distance between (yards)	Δ from mean = Distance − 544 (yards)	ΣΔ from mean (yards)	Distance between (metres)	Δ from mean = Distance − 497 (metres)	ΣΔ from mean (metres)
TURRET 7B TO TURRET 10A						
7B – 8	710	166	+166	649	152	+152
8 – 8A	522	-22	+144	477	-20	+132
8A – 8B	532	-12	+132	486	-11	+121
8B – 9	548	4	+136	501	4	+125
9 – 9B	1063	Av. −12.5 x 2	+111	972	Av. −11.5 x 2	+102
9B – 10	545	1	+112	498	1	+103
10 – 10A	509	-35	+77	465	-32	+71
MILECASTLE 22 TO MILECASTLE 27						
22 – 22A	539	-5	-5	493	-5	-5
22A – 22B	540	-4	-9	494	-4	-8
22B – 23	543	-1	-10	497	-1	-9

Milecastle and Turret No.	Distance between (yards)	Δ from mean = Distance − 544 (yards)	ΣΔ from mean (yards)	Distance between (metres)	Δ from mean = Distance − 497 (metres)	ΣΔ from mean (metres)
23 – 23A	543	-1	-11	497	-1	-10
23A – 23B	542	-2	-13	496	-2	-12
23B – 24	533	-11	-24	487	-10	-22
24 – 24A	539	-5	-29	493	-5	-27
24A – 24B	541	-3	-32	495	-3	-29
24B – 25	553	9	-23	506	8	-21
25 – 25A	553	9	-14	506	8	-13
25A – 25B	551	7	-7	504	6	-6
25B – 26	544	0	-7	497	0	-6
26 – 26A	535	-9	-16	489	-8	-15
26A – 26B	550	6	-10	503	5	-9
26B – 27	552	8	-2	505	7	-2
MILECASTLE 29 TO MILECASTLE 31						
29 – 29A	534	-10	-10	488	-9	-9
29A – 29B	534	-10	-20	488	-9	-18
29B – 30	528	-16	-36	483	-15	-33
30 – 30A	594	50	+14	543	46	+13
30A – 30B	539	-5	+9	493	-5	+8
30B – 31	529	-15	-6	484	-14	-5
MILECASTLE 36 TO MILECASTLE 42						
36 – 36A	509	-35	-35	465	-32	-32
36A – 37	1159	Av. 35.5 x 2	+36	1060	Av. 32.5 x 2	+33
37 – 37A	532	-12	+24	486	-11	+22
37A – 37B	537	-7	+17	491	-6	+16
37B – 38	535	-9	+8	489	-8	+7

Milecastle and Turret No.	Distance between (yards)	Δ from mean = Distance – 544 (yards)	ΣΔ from mean (yards)	Distance between (metres)	Δ from mean = Distance – 497 (metres)	ΣΔ from mean (metres)
38 – 38A	549	5	+13	502	5	+12
38A – 38B	535	-9	+4	489	-8	+4
38B – 39	445	-99	-95	406	-91	-87
39 – 39A	513	-31	-126	469	-28	-115
39A – 39B	767	223	+97	701	204	+89
39B – 40	526	-18	+79	481	-16	+72
40 – 40A	624	80	+159	571	73	+145
40A – 40B	642	98	+257	587	90	+235
40B – 41	584	40	+297	534	37	+272
41 – 41A	582	38	+335	532	35	+306
41A – 41B	501	-43	+292	458	-39	+267
41B – 42	558	14	+306	510	13	+280
TURRET 43A TO MILECASTLE 46						
43A – 43B	555	11	+11	507	10	+10
43B – 44	537	-7	+4	491	-6	+4
44 – 44A	574	30	+34	525	27	+31
44A – 44B	395	-149	-115	361	-136	-105
44B – 45	552	8	-107	505	7	-98
45 – 45A	447	-97	-204	409	-89	-187
45A – 45B	578	34	-170	529	31	-155
45B – 46	566	22	-148	518	20	-135
MILECASTLE 47 TO TURRET 51B						
47 – 47A	540	-4	-4	494	-4	-4
47A – 47B	546	2	-2	499	2	-2
47B – 48	578	34	+32	529	31	+29

Milecastle and Turret No.	Distance between (yards)	Δ from mean = Distance – 544 (yards)	ΣΔ from mean (yards)	Distance between (metres)	Δ from mean = Distance – 497 (metres)	ΣΔ from mean (metres)
48 – 48A	498	-46	-14	455	-42	-13
48A – 48B	533	-11	-25	487	-10	-23
48B – 49	564	20	-5	516	18	-5
49 – 49B (stone wall)	997	Av.-45.5 x 2	-96	912	Av. –41.5 x 2	-88
49B – 50 (stone wall)	541	-3	-99	495	-3	-91
50 – 50A (stone wall)	544	0	-99	497	0	-91
50A – 50B (stone wall)	540	-4	-103	494	-4	-94
50B (stone wall) – 51	545	1	-102	498	1	-93
51 – 51A	547	3	-99	500	3	-90
51A – 51B	530	-14	-113	485	-13	-103

ANALYSIS AND DISCUSSION

There are three ways of measuring the distance between two points along a wall which is not straight:

a) directly between the points, i.e. as the crow flies;
b) measuring along the line of the wall horizontally, as though on a map;
c) measuring along the line of the wall following the ground, with its ups and downs in between.

Collingwood does not state which way he used. It can be imagined that the Roman surveyors would have used c), although we have no proof of this. On common sense grounds, it seems likely that Collingwood would have used either b) or c), and fortunately experiment shows that the differences between measurements made by either b) or c) are usually slight unless there should be exceptionally steep inclines or declines between any two points.

An attempt was made to compare Collingwood's figures with the positions of the turrets and milecastles that are printed on the 1975 Ordnance Survey Map of Hadrian's Wall, but no exact correspondence was found. Sometimes the spacings on the Ordnance Survey Map appeared to be greater than Collingwood's, and sometimes less. This is not to assume that the Ordnance Survey Map (which was published forty or more years after Collingwood's measurements were made) is necessarily the more accurate of the two, but it does mean that there must be an element of uncertainty about the accuracy of Collingwood's figures. Nevertheless, Collingwood's data is what we have, and so it is worth analysing what conclusions we may be able to draw from it.

At least one conclusion can be drawn from the data. One way in which the Romans might have fixed the locations of their milecastles and turrets would have been for the surveyors to have marked out in advance the exact theoretically spaced positions along the line of Hadrian's Wall, and then left it to the construction teams to vary the positions laterally in each case, in order to adapt them to local circumstances when the time came to build them. If this had been the case, then the accumulated displacements (i.e. column 4 in the table) can be expected to converge upon some constant close to zero. This is because the displacements to either side of the mean, which in response to the topography can be expected to have been essentially random and equally distributed to either side of it, would have cancelled each other out in due course as the number of milecastles and turrets in our samples increased. As can be seen, there is little overall evidence of this. In places the accumulated displacement continues to grow over considerable lengths of the line of the Wall, which seems to rule out this way of setting-out. Rather, it appears to me to indicate a sequential method of working, in which those planning the positions of the milecastles and turrets simply proceeded from one chosen location to select the next.

There are, however, abrupt changes in the accumulated displacements at certain locations, including:

- between turret 39A and turret 39B;
- between milecastle 40 and turret 40B;
- between turret 44A and turret 44B;
- and, to a lesser extent, between milecastle 45 and turret 45A;
- and another may have occurred between turret 7B and milecastle 8.

It could be that the Romans had divided up the spacing-out of the milecastles and turrets along Hadrian's Wall into separate sectors, and that these abrupt changes in the accumulated displacements reflect where the sectors met. However, to have adopted this tactic – effectively of starting from more than one datum point – would almost inevitably have caused problems with discontinuities in the spacing, and this would have been obvious to the Roman before they started. Hence I am inclined to discard this possible explanation as unlikely.

Another possibility is that some of the turrets along Hadrian's Wall may have been in existence as pre-Wall towers, like those at Pike Hill and Birdoswald, and that the Romans' intentions had been to incorporate them into the line of the Wall. Turret 45A, for instance, is believed to have been such a pre-Wall tower, and it is interesting to note that this is where one of the discontinuities occurs.

Trying to fit such pre-existing towers into a newly imposed rigid system of spacing would be almost certain to cause mismatches and discontinuities in the spacing. It is therefore possible that the Roman surveyors consciously sought to minimise such discontinuities (or possibly even to disguise them) by deliberately increasing or decreasing the mean spacing between their milecastles and turrets as they approached such pre-Wall structures. The Romans may have appreciated that a variation in spacing of 50 yards or so within 500 yards is unlikely to be noticed by an observer on the ground, especially if the variation is sustained for several milecastles and turrets in a row, whereas a discontinuity of 100 yards or more between two such structures would probably have been very noticeable. Hence it could be worth investigating if turrets 7B, 39A or B, 40A or B, and 44A or B might have been pre-Wall towers. Against this hypothesis, however, it should be noted that when Pike Hill tower was incorporated into Hadrian's Wall, it was left outside the regular system of spacing of turrets and milecastles. The system ignored the existing tower at Pike Hill, running past it and positioning another turret, 52A, only 200 yards or so (c.200 m) to the west of it (see Plate 24).

For individual milecastles and turrets, it can be imagined that their displacements from a theoretically calculated position could have been for a variety of physical reasons. For instance, the theoretically correct position of a turret or milecastle might have been on unsuitable ground, or too close to or even at the bottom of a ravine, or else there may have been a military need to overlook a natural route of incursion. Nevertheless the size of some of the displacements suggests that there may have been larger factors at work. One of these could well have been David Woolliscroft's proposition that the positions of many of the milecastles and turrets, in the central sector of Hadrian's Wall at least, had been adjusted so that they could signal to the forts and fortlets along the line of the Stanegate road to the rear.[2] But the possibility that there might have been more pre-Wall towers than is currently appreciated may be worthy of further consideration too. If these had had to be fitted in as unobtrusively as possible when a scheme of nominally regular spacing of the milecastles and turrets was imposed, it could help to explain the growths in the accumulated displacements of the turrets and milecastles over considerable lengths of the Wall which is evident in the data, as noted and discussed above.

Other factors may also remain to be diagnosed. As remarked in Chapter 11, one of the purposes of presenting this data and analysis here is to allow others to see if they can extract information from the material that might have eluded me. In addition, new digital technologies may now allow the distances along the ground between the milecastles and turrets to be established more accurately and certainly than R. G. Collingwood was able to do, and thus provide researchers with a much more firm and precise set of data for analyses of this kind.

---

2   Woolliscroft 2001, 63-7.

REFERENCES

CHAPTER 1

Breeze, D. J. 1969-70. 'Excavations at Ardoch 1970', *Proceedings of the Society of Antiquaries of Scotland*, 102: 122-8.

Hodge, A. T. 1995. *Roman Aqueducts & Water Supply*. First published 1991, reprinted 1995. London, Gerald Duckworth & Co. Ltd.

Hodgson, N. (ed.) 2009. *Hadrian's Wall 1999-2009: A Summary of Excavation and Research prepared for the Thirteenth Pilgrimage of Hadrian's Wall, 8-14 August 2009*. Kendal, The Cumberland and Westmorland Antiquarian and Archaeological Society and The Society of Antiquaries of Newcastle upon Tyne.

Lewis, M. J. T. 2001. *Surveying Instruments of Greece and Rome*. Cambridge, Cambridge University Press.

Margary, I. D. 1973. *Roman Roads in Britain*. Third edition. London, John Baker Publishers Ltd.

CHAPTER 2

Campbell, B. 2000. *The Writings of the Roman Land Surveyors: Introduction, Text, Translations, Commentary*. London, Society for the Promotion of Roman Studies.

Davies, H. E. H. 1998. 'Designing Roman roads', *Britannia*, 29: 1-16.

Davies, H. E. H. 2002. *Roads in Roman Britain*. Stroud, Tempus Publishing Ltd.

Lewis, M. J. T. 2001. *Surveying Instruments of Greece and Rome*. Cambridge, Cambridge University Press.

In addition, the following references are provided by Arnaud Bertrand in support of the development of a model for the typical pattern of conquest, derived from the expansion of the Western Han Empire into Xinjiang province in China:

1. Chun-shu Chang, *Military Aspects of Han Wu-ti's Northern and Northwestern Compaigns*, Harvard Journal of Asiatic Studies 26, 1966, p.148-173.

2. Chun-shu Chang, *Qin-Han China in Review: The Field, New Frontiers, and Next Assignment, Studies in Chinese History* 4, 1994, p.47-59.

3. Chun-shu Chang, *The Rise of the Chinese Empire*, 2 Vol., University of Michigan Press, 2007.

4. Chun-shu Chang, "War and Peace with the Hsiungnu in Early Han China: The Hsiungnu Challenge (200-133 BC) and the origins of the Han Wu-ti's Military Expansion", in *Essays in Commemoration of the Eigthieth Birthday of Professor T'ao His-sheng*, Taipei: Shih-huo ch'u-pan she, 1979, p. 611-698.

5. Chun-shu Chang, "Ku-tai t'un-tien chih-tu te yuan-shih yü Hsi-han Hohsi Hsi-yü pien-sai shang t'un-t'ien chih-tu chih fa-chan kuo-ch'eng" (The Origins of the Agricultural Colony System and China's Establishment of It in the Frontier Regions of Ho-his and His-yü [The Western Regions]), in *Ch'ü Wan-li hsien-sheng ch'i-chih jung-ch'ing lun-wei chi*, Taipei, Lien-ching, 1978, pp. 563-599.

CHAPTER 4

Bidwell, P. and Hodgson, N. 2009. *The Roman Army in Northern England*. South Shields, The Arbeia Society on behalf of the Organising Committee of the XXIst International *Limes* (Roman Frontiers Studies) Congress, Newcastle upon Tyne.

Bishop, M. C. 2005. 'A New Flavian Military Site at Roecliffe, North Yorkshire', *Britannia*, 36: 135-223.

Clarke, S. 2007. *Roman Dere Street and the Road Network Around Newstead Fort*. Unpublished draft report 29–06–07.

Cool, H. E. M. and Mason, David J. P. (eds) 2008. *Roman Piercebridge: Excavations by D. W. Harding and Peter Scott 1969–1981*. Research Report 7. Durham, The Architectural and Archaeological Society of Durham and Northumberland.

Poulter, J. 2009. *Surveying Roman Military Landscapes across Northern Britain: the Planning of Roman Dere Street, Hadrian's Wall and the Vallum, and the Antonine Wall in Scotland* with a supplementary report *Mapping Matters with the Antonine Wall* by Peter McKeague. British Archaeological Reports 492, Oxford, Archaeopress.

Vindolanda Tablets Online. http://vindolanda.csad.ox.ac.uk Tablet 343 (88.946).

CHAPTER 5

Bidwell, P. T. and Holbrook, N. 1989. *Hadrian's Wall Bridges*. London, Historic Buildings & Monuments Commission for England.

Boucher, C. T. G. 1963. *John Rennie 1761-1821: the Life and Work of a Great Engineer*. Manchester, Manchester University Press.

Breeze, D. J. 2006. *Handbook to the Roman Wall*, fourteenth edition. Newcastle upon Tyne, The Society of Antiquaries of Newcastle upon Tyne.

Dymond, D. P. 1961. 'Roman Bridges on Dere Street, County Durham', *Archaeological Journal*, 118: 136-64.

O'Connor, C. 1993. *Roman Bridges*. Cambridge, Cambridge University Press.

Poulter, J. 1998. 'The date of the Stanegate, and a hypothesis about the manner and timing of the construction of Roman roads in Britain', *Archaeologia Aeliana*, fifth series, 26: 49-58.

Poulter, J. 2005. 'Linear Legacies: the disappearance of closed transport routes, as illustrated by the Midland Counties Railway line between Rugby and Leicester', *Journal of the Railway & Canal Historical Society*, 192: 79-85.

CHAPTER 6

Allan, M. 1994. *The Roman Route across the Northern Lake District: Brougham to Moresby*. Lancaster, Centre for North-West Regional Studies, University of Lancaster.

Davies, H. E. H. 2002. *Roads in Roman Britain*. Stroud, Tempus Publishing Ltd.

Graystone, P. 2002. *Walking Roman Roads in Lonsdale and the Eden Valley*. Lancaster, Centre for North-West Regional Studies, University of Lancaster.

Hale, D. *et al.* 2007. 'Archaeology on the Otterburn Training Area, 2002-2005', *Archaeologia Aeliana*, fifth series, 36: 31-77.

Hart, C. R. 1984. *The North Derbyshire Archaeological Survey*. Sheffield, The Derbyshire Archaeological Society, reprinted on behalf of Sheffield City Museums.

Margary, I. D. 1973, *Roman Roads in Britain*. Third edition. London, John Baker Publishers Ltd.

Selkirk, R. 1995. *On the Trail of the Legions*. Ipswich, Anglia.

Simco, A. 1984. *Survey of Bedfordshire: the Roman Period*. Bedford, Bedfordshire County Council and the Royal Commission on Historical Monuments (England).

The *Viatores* 1964. *Roman Roads in the South-East Midlands*. London, Victor Gollancz.

Waddelove, E. 1999. *The Roman Roads of North Wales: recent discoveries*. Ruthin, Denbighshire, published privately by the author.

Watkins, A. 1972. *The Old Straight Track*. First published 1925, reprinted 1970 and 1972. London, Garnstone Press Ltd.

Williamson, T. and Bellamy, L. 1983. *Ley lines in question*. Tadworth, Surrey, World's Work Ltd.

CHAPTER 7

Lawson, A. B. 2006. *A Country called Stratherrick*. Second edition. Stratherrick, South Loch Ness Heritage Group.

Taylor, W. 1996. *The Military Roads of Scotland*. Revised edition. Isle of Colonsay, Argyll, House of Lochar.

CHAPTER 8

Poulter, J. 2009. *Surveying Roman Military Landscapes across Northern Britain: the Planning of Roman Dere Street, Hadrian's Wall and the Vallum, and the Antonine Wall in Scotland* with a supplementary report *Mapping Matters with the*

Antonine Wall by Peter McKeague. British Archaeological Reports 492, Oxford, Archaeopress.

CHAPTER 9

Bidwell, P. 2003. 'The original terminus of Hadrian's Wall', *Archaeologia Aeliana*, fifth series, 32: 17–24.

Biggins, J. A., Hall, S. and Taylor, D. J. A. 2004. 'A geophysical survey of Milecastle 73 and Hadrian's Wall at Burgh-by-Sands, Cumbria', *Transactions of the Cumberland and Westmorland Archaeological and Antiquarian Society*, third series, 4: 55-70.

Breeze, D. J. and Hill, P. R. 2001. 'Hadrian's Wall began here', *Archaeologia Aeliana*, fifth series, 29: 1–2.

Breeze, D. J. 2006. *Handbook to the Roman Wall*, fourteenth edition. Newcastle upon Tyne, The Society of Antiquaries of Newcastle upon Tyne.

Haverfield, F. 1900. 'Report of the Cumberland Excavation Committee for 1899', *Transactions of the Cumberland and Westmorland Archaeological and Antiquarian Society* first series, 16: 80-99.

Hill, P. R. 2001. 'Hadrian's Wall from MC0 to MC9', *Archaeologia Aeliana*, fifth series, 29: 3-18.

Hill, P. R. 2006. *The Construction of Hadrian's Wall*. Stroud, Tempus Publishing Ltd.

Ordnance Survey 1975. *Map of Hadrian's Wall, Scale 2 Inches to 1 Mile*. Second edition 1972, updated in 1975. Southampton.

Poulter, J. 2008. 'The direction of planning of the eastern sector of Hadrian's Wall: some further thoughts', in Bidwell P. (ed.), *Understanding Hadrian's Wall*, 99-104. South Shields, The Arbeia Society.

Poulter, J. 2009. *Surveying Roman Military Landscapes across Northern Britain: the Planning of Roman Dere Street, Hadrian's Wall and the Vallum, and the Antonine Wall in Scotland* with a supplementary report *Mapping Matters with the Antonine Wall* by Peter McKeague. British Archaeological Reports 492, Oxford, Archaeopress.

Woolliscroft, D. J. 2001. *Roman Military Signalling*. Stroud, Tempus Publishing Ltd.

CHAPTER 10

Checkland, P. and Poulter, J. 2006. *Learning for Action: A Short Definitive Account of Soft Systems Methodology and its use for Practitioners, Teachers and Students*. Chichester, John Wiley & Sons Ltd.

Poulter, J. 1998. 'The date of the Stanegate, and a hypothesis about the manner and timing of the construction of Roman roads in Britain', *Archaeologia Aeliana*, fifth series, 26: 49–58.

Woolliscroft, D. J. and Hoffmann, B. 2006. *Rome's First Frontier: The Flavian Occupation of Northern Scotland*. Stroud, Tempus Publishing Ltd.

CHAPTER 11

Breeze, D. J. 2006. *Handbook to the Roman Wall*, fourteenth edition. Newcastle upon Tyne, The Society of Antiquaries of Newcastle upon Tyne.

Breeze, D. J. 2009. 'Did Hadrian design Hadrian's Wall?', *Archaeologia Aeliana*, fifth series, 38: 87-103.

Breeze, D. J. and Woolliscroft, D. J. 2009. *Excavation and Survey at Roman Burgh-by-Sands*. Carlisle, The Cumberland and Westmorland Antiquarian and Archaeological Society.

Poulter, J. 2009. *Surveying Roman Military Landscapes across Northern Britain: the Planning of Roman Dere Street, Hadrian's Wall and the Vallum, and the Antonine Wall in Scotland* with a supplementary report *Mapping Matters with the Antonine Wall* by Peter McKeague. British Archaeological Reports 492, Oxford, Archaeopress.

Symonds, M. F. A. and Mason, D. J. P. (eds) 2009. *Frontiers of Knowledge: a research framework for Hadrian's Wall*. Volume 1: resource assessment. Durham, Durham County Council.

Woolliscroft, D. J. 2001. *Roman Military Signalling*. Stroud, Tempus Publishing Ltd.

Woolliscroft, D. J. 2002. *The Roman Frontier on the Gask Ridge: Perth and Kinross*. British Archaeological Reports 335, Oxford, Archaeopress.

CHAPTER 12

Hanson, W. S. and Maxwell, G. S. 1986. *Rome's North West Frontier*. Second edition. Edinburgh, Edinburgh University Press.

Hodgson, N. (ed.) 2009. *Hadrian's Wall 1999-2009: A Summary of Excavation and Research prepared for the Thirteenth Pilgrimage of Hadrian's Wall, 8-14 August 2009*. Kendal, The Cumberland and Westmorland Antiquarian and Archaeological Society and The Society of Antiquaries of Newcastle upon Tyne.

RCAHMS 2007. *Frontiers of the Roman Empire World Heritage Site: The Antonine Wall: Proposed Extension, 1:5000 series maps*. Edinburgh, Historic Scotland.

RCAHMS 2008. *The Antonine Wall, 1:25,000 map*. Edinburgh, The Royal Commission on the Ancient and Historical Monuments of Scotland.

Robertson, A. S. and Keppie, L. 2001. *The Antonine Wall: A handbook to the surviving remains*. Fifth edition. Glasgow, Glasgow Archaeological Society.

Swan, V. G. 1999. 'The Twentieth Legion and the history of the Antonine Wall reconsidered', *Proceedings of the Society of Antiquaries of Scotland*, 129: 399-480.

Woolliscroft, D. J. 1996. 'Signalling and the design of the Antonine Wall', *Britannia*, 27: 153–77.

Woolliscroft, D. J. 2008. 'Excavations at Garnhall on the line of the Antonine Wall', *Proceedings of the Society of Antiquaries of Scotland*, 138: 129-76.

APPENDIX

Collingwood, R. G. 1929-30. 'Hadrian's Wall – A system of numerical references', *Proceedings of the Society of Antiquaries of Newcastle upon Tyne*, fourth series, 4: 179-87.

Woolliscroft, D. J. 2001. *Roman Military Signalling*. Stroud, Tempus Publishing Ltd.

INDEX